T0164471

Kwame Nkrumah

Kwame Nkrumah

The Father
of
African Nationalism

Revised Edition

David Birmingham

Ohio University Press

ATHENS

Ohio University Press, Athens, Ohio 45701
© 1998, 1990 by David Birmingham

Revised edition published by Ohio University Press, 1998.
First edition, under the title *Kwame Nkrumah* in the Makers of
the Twentieth Century series, published in Great Britain by
Sphere Books Ltd., 1990.

Ohio University Press books are printed on acid-free paper ⊖"

02 01 00 99 98 5 4 3 2 1

The chapter "Nkrumah in Retirement" appeared in slightly different form in
*Threefold Wisdom: Islam, the Arab World, and Africa. Papers in Honour of
Ivan Hrbek*, edited by Otakar Hulec and Milos Mendel (Prague: Academy of
Sciences of the Czech Republic, Oriental Institute, 1993).

Cover photograph reproduced from Willis E. Bell, *Ghana on the Move.*

Library of Congress Cataloging-in-Publication Data

Birmingham, David
    Kwame Nkrumah : the father of African nationalism /
David Birmingham. — Rev. ed.
        p.   cm.
    The first ed., without subtitle, was published: London : Sphere Books,
1990, in the series: Makers of the twentieth century.
    Includes bibliographical references and indes.
    ISBN 0-8214-1242-6 (paper : alk. paper)
    1. Nkrumah, Kwame, 1909-1972. 2. Presidents — Ghana — Biography.
3. Ghana — Politics and governmant — 1957-1979. 4. Nationalism — Africa —
History — 20th century. 5. Pan-Africanism. I. Title.
DT512.3.N57B53   1998
966.705′092 — dc21
    [b]   98-7888
                                                            CIP

For Walter and Maisie Birmingham

CONTENTS

PREFACE TO
THE REVISED EDITION

The first edition of this biography was published in 1990, almost twenty years after Kwame Nkrumah had died. At the time it was possible to provide a reasonably evenhanded assessment of his public career. The extremes of adulation and denigration had slipped into the shadows and Nkrumah emerged as a man of both strength and weakness who had achieved much on the national plane while at the same time being defeated in some of his international ambitions. The limitation of the first edition of this book, however, was in its assessment of Nkrumah as a private man. This weakness can now be partially remedied by new evidence that has come into the public domain.

After Nkrumah left the public scene he went into a rather reclusive exile at Conakry in the French-speaking West African republic of Guinea. Although he received few visitors, he did maintain an extensive correspondence during his retirement, and a selection of his letters has been published by June Milne. They form the basis of a new final chapter to this book. In his retirement he maintained contact with world leaders who recognized him for the visionary that he was. The sadness of his final years was marked, however, by a failure to come to terms with his domestic record. In Ghana a reevaluation of his path as a statesman had to await another generation. Meanwhile Nkrumah himself believed to the last that his country might call him back to serve in the struggle against the foreign influences that were creeping into Africa during the postcolonial era.

The most revealing aspect of Nkrumah's retirement was the light it shed on his engagingly boyish personality. His old enthusiasms were revitalized when the burdens of office were lifted from him. But the shyness was still there, and it is his reticence that emerges as a strong feature of his personality in a second major source published since the first edition of this biography. Nkrumah the private man, as opposed to Nkrumah the world statesman, has been newly portrayed by the researches of Marika Sherwood. Her book, *Kwame Nkrumah: The Years Abroad, 1935-1947*, has uncovered a wealth of information about Nkrumah's long years in, and on the fringes of, the world of student politics.

The picture that new research reveals of Nkrumah in prewar America is of a complex and contradictory man who was no longer so young by student standards. He was jovial but studious, shy but ambitious, disorganized but persistent, and his friends claimed that despite his reticence and introspection he was "friendly in a distant sort of way." In ten years he gained four degrees, one in sociology, one in "sacred theology," one in education, and one in philosophy, but he never gained the doctorate in political science that he craved. He avoided the hurly-burly of student activism but showed solidarity with his fellow Africans by supporting their soccer team in the role of referee.

When Nkrumah arrived in Britain as a student-turned-politician he continued — as he did throughout his life — to have difficulty in writing. His first foray into journalism with *The New African* was not a success, his thesis was never completed, and even his famous pamphlet, *Towards Colonial Freedom*, was published in 1947 only with the hidden help of a press subsidized by the Communist Party.

It was only when Nkrumah arrived back in Africa that his magic touch began to blossom. There, in an oral culture rather than a literary one, he found his vocation. The shy student became the master of the political arts, a conversationalist who could charm all who dealt with him, a speechmaker who could enthrall the crowds, and eventually a leader who could inspire Africa to shed the colonial yoke.

Canterbury, 18 December 1997

CHRONOLOGY

1909   Probable year of birth

1935   Arrived in America for a stay of ten years

1945   Helped organize the Manchester Conference on
        Pan-Africanism

1947   Appointed Secretary of the United Gold Coast Convention

1949   Founded the Convention People's Party

1951   Won the first Gold Coast general election

1956   Won the independence election

1957   Gained Ghana independence as a Commonwealth dominion

1958   Hosted the All-Africa People's Conference in Accra

1960   Elected first president of the Republic of Ghana

1963   Participated in the founding of the Organization of
        African Unity

1966   Overthrown in a police-army *coup d'état*

1972   Died of cancer after a six-year exile in Guinea

I

Black Apprentice

In May 1945, a few days after war ended in Europe, a penniless
black graduate sailed out of New York. Kwame Nkrumah was returning to the Old World after ten years in the United States. Two
years later he arrived back in his native Africa and four years after that
became "Leader of Government Business" in the newly created parliament of the Gold Coast. He was on his way to becoming the first black
prime minister of a modern democracy. His success heralded a trans-
formation of the face of Africa. In little more than a decade colonial
governments gave way to independent ones in all but the five white-
dominated states of Africa's deep south. The Gold Coast, rechristened
Ghana, led a cohort of the thirty-five African countries into the United
Nations. Black people everywhere began to walk tall. The name of
Nkrumah became familiar across the world.

The three threads which ran through Nkrumah's career were the
concept of black identity, the search for national autonomy, and the
advocacy of Pan-African unity. All three were constant themes in his
political thinking, but their relative importance was in chronological

sequence. Black consciousness was the first to surface, in the 1940s, while he was a student in the white Anglo-Saxon world. It ceased to be so important when he returned to Africa and Nkrumah never became a black racist. He worked effectively with British advisers, married a Coptic wife, cooperated with North African Arabs, and was host to liberal white exiles from South Africa. At the same time he became the hero of movements that did have blackness as their unifying symbolism. Black Power, however, became more radical than Nkrumah himself as he redirected his energies to the national affairs of his own territory.

Independence as a national goal dominated the 1950s and brought Nkrumah his greatest successes and his most unqualified acclaim. His drive and imagination, his idealism and energy, blended perfectly with the more sober practical and organizational skills of his accomplices. Between them, he and his lieutenants created a mass party and won their national freedom. They did so according to the shifting democratic rules that Britain from time to time imposed in the hope of shaping the new Ghana to suit its own interests. Self-government was won in 1951, independent dominion status followed in 1957, and the republican constitution was declared in 1960. President Nkrumah was able to welcome the British Queen to Africa in the most gracious style and with a hospitality that radiated his own inimitable laughter.

The third phase of Nkrumah's career, the 1960s, was dominated by a desire to see the rest of Africa liberated from colonial and settler domination. The colonial rulers were seen off, but the settlers were not. The big disappointment, however, was that the new ex-colonial states prided themselves on their national identities and showed no inclination to subordinate their independence to a wider ideal of Pan-African unity. Former colonies followed Nkrumah's example by winning freedom but failed to heed his call for African solidarity and resistance to neocolonial manipulation. Only after his fall from office in 1966, and his death in 1972, did Africa begin to realize how prophetic his warnings against neocolonialism had been. Like Simon Bolivar, the liberator of South America, Kwame Nkrumah became the posthumous hero of a balkanized continent.

Student Abroad

Nkrumah had been born about 1909 in the southwestern corner of Ghana. Over the previous fifteen years British troops from the old merchant territories of the Gold Coast colony had invaded the once powerful empire of Asante and imposed British "protection" over those parts of its hinterland which had not already been staked out by armed columns of French and German soldiers from adjacent colonies. In these early colonial years the British presence was slight, but Nkrumah happened to live within the sphere of a Catholic mission which provided him with schooling. His mother saved the necessary coins for his school fees and expenses. She was the dominant influence on his life in the absence of his itinerant father. In the retiring simplicity of her village Nkrumah's mother watched over him throughout his life and for a while guarded his tomb after his death.

Nkrumah's career as a trainee schoolmaster in the 1930s took him to a teachers' college adjoining the then new government public school of Achimota. Seven miles away, at Accra, lay the colonial capital which had been moved from the old fortress town of Cape Coast. Accra consisted of three ancient trade castles on a sweeping beach served by carved surf boats which ferried people and goods through the breakers to ships anchored on the open sea. The town was scattered, but it was the place in which to meet intellectuals and exiles, journalists and lawyers, idealists and administrators. One of the men who most excited Nkrumah in this miniature world of heady cosmopolitan ideas was Nnamdi Azikiwe, later to be president of Nigeria. He set to thinking about studying overseas rather than devoting the rest of his life to being a Catholic schoolmaster. When he failed to gain matriculation to the University of London he followed Azikiwe's example, borrowed money from a generous family network, and set out for America in search of an alternative education.

Nkrumah reached the United States in 1935 to begin working his way through Lincoln, a black university in Pennsylvania. Life was burdened with dishwashing in restaurant sculleries, but on Sundays he visited black Presbyterian churches in Philadelphia and New York. When invited to be a guest preacher he discovered that his powers of oratory could enthrall his congregations. Preaching in the Protestant style enhanced his frail self-confidence and provided the spiritual security and emotional stimulus that he needed. During his ten-year career as a student Nkrumah read politics as well as divinity and encountered the ideas of Marcus Garvey, who had been a radical Jamaican living in the United States. Most black Americans aspired to be accepted into the broad stream of achievement-oriented American life, but Garvey created a movement that looked toward Africa for a different future with a black empire on the soil of the ancestors. To a lonely African, swallowed up in American poverty, the idealized visions of Garvey were like manna from heaven. Nkrumah's reading went beyond politics and for a time he earned an income from tutoring students in philosophy. This apparently brought him into contact with another great Caribbean writer, C. L. R. James of Trinidad. James did not have a high regard for Nkrumah's academic abilities, but in 1945 nevertheless commended him, albeit patronizingly, to the attention of the black expatriate community in Britain.

Ten years of living overseas profoundly affected Nkrumah's temperament. Despite his lifelong reputation as a lone man, he does nevertheless seem to have made friends in America. One of them was a

Gold Coast law student, Ako Adjei, with whom he tried to organize student politics among the few Africans living on the eastern seaboard. Adjei subsequently helped to advance Nkrumah's political career, though they later quarreled painfully. Some of Nkrumah's American friends were women and for the rest of his life Nkrumah usually felt more at ease in the company of women than he did with men. No psychologist has ever speculated on what latent streak of personality enabled Nkrumah to relate more freely and creatively to women than he did to men, but his relationship with women does not seem to have been based, as his critics liked to believe, on an unbridled sexual appetite, but rather on a broader and deeper companionship. In later years, when fame had caught up with him, Nkrumah revisited Philadelphia and sought out some of his old friends. But for all the support he received from churches and colleges, from companions and colleagues, the life of a black exile in the northern cities of America was hard, even when the great recession of the 1930s gave way to fuller wartime employment. Waiting to go home and failing to achieve academic distinction were bitter experiences.

Interlude in Britain
Nkrumah arrived in Britain in 1945 and appears to have been welcomed into a slightly more congenial social milieu than the American one. He was accepted into a community of Caribbean activists who helped him find Spartan digs with a sympathetic landlady during the chronic housing shortage. The life of a black student in postwar London was graphically portrayed in the novel *Stormy Dawn,* written pseudonymously under the name Mark Freshfield by one of Nkrumah's later associates, and Peter Abraham's *Wreath for Udomo* also captured the age. Nkrumah found that the scope for mobilizing students into thinking about the future of colonialism was a little wider than in

America, though student politics were austere and the office stove had to be fed on stray lumps of coal gleaned in the cold, depressed gutters of London. Black students gained a certain cachet with some radical whites and could depend on a circle of admirers to help with organizing, typing, and maintaining morale. The life of exile was otherwise devoted to endless speculative talk about the problems of racism, and the prospects of freedom, while nursing dead tea cups in linoleum cafés.

One important highlight brightened this cold world of waiting. It was a conference held in Manchester in the autumn of 1945. Thomas Griffiths, a radical Guyanese café owner who had adopted the "Abyssinian" name of Makonnen, invited leaders of the movements for colonial freedom to Manchester with the lure of subsidized meals in his restaurants. The Manchester gathering became known as the Fifth Pan-African Conference. The concept of Pan-Africanism came from the black Diaspora in the Americas and especially from the West Indian intellectual élite. The rival ideological patrons were Marcus Garvey, whose widow attended, and W. E. B. Du Bois, the veteran African-American who presided in person. The fourth Pan-African conference had been held in New York in 1927, though the roots of the movement were also to be found in earlier meetings held in London and Paris, Lisbon and Brussels. African awareness of this Pan-African concept was slight but it had been enhanced by the Italian invasion of Ethiopia in 1935, even though the exiled emperor seems to have rather cold-shouldered the black radicals who tried to visit his English court at Bath. Africans from six colonies, all of them anglophone, took part in the Manchester assembly, but the driving force was the Trinidadian activist George Padmore, formerly known as Malcolm Nurse. His assistant, beavering away in the back-room, was Kwame Nkrumah, formerly known as Francis Nkrumah.

The Manchester conference was seminal in fostering an interna-

tional ground swell of black aspiration and solidarity. Some participants, such as Jomo Kenyatta, formerly known as Johnstone, were
already mildly famous. For Nkrumah this was a first exposure to stage
politics and the conference had a style that he was to make his own.
More than that, the message from Manchester was indelibly stamped
on Nkrumah's career. It exhorted the exiles to go forth and liberate
their home territories in order to make way for the unification of
Africa. Much mythology later accrued to the Manchester conference
both in the black power movement and in Pan-African circles, but
whatever else it did or did not do, it certainly helped to launch
Nkrumah as an apprentice politician. Nkrumah became the most successful of all George Padmore's protégés and Padmore subsequently
became one of the closest and most trusted of Nkrumah's political
advisers. Padmore's death in 1959 coincided, perhaps not altogether
fortuitously, with the apogee of Nkrumah's career.

The experience which Padmore was able to give Nkrumah as a
political activist and publicity organizer had been partly gained in the
Soviet Union. He advised aspiring politicians to study communist, even
Stalinist, methods without being caught by communist organizations, to
get a party card but to take care not to sign it. Padmore was a good
teacher, though he probably retained a personal faith in violence while
Nkrumah's African liberation movement became firmly wedded to the
Gandhian ideal of nonviolence. In private Padmore's wit could be mor-
dant: "White man make a revolution, he shoot and proclaim the soviets;
black man make a revolution, he say: 'Mr. Governor, suh, will you please
convene a constituent assembly.'" But Padmore's chief contribution to
Nkrumah's maturation was not a belief in armed violence, but an idealized commitment to African unity as the only way out of the poverty of
colonial fragmentation. That ideal became Nkrumah's own and was his
lifelong crusade. Manchester had set him on his way.

Rediscovering Africa

It was in the autumn of 1947 that Nkrumah was presented with an opportunity to embark on a political career. He was invited to become the general secretary of a political convention then being set up on the Gold Coast to explore the paths to independence. The invitation came from a caucus of lawyers, chiefs, businessmen and intellectuals to whom Nkrumah had been commended by his student associate of American days, Ako Adjei. Nkrumah's qualification for the job derived from his experience as a student organizer in London rather than from his radical political views. Indeed it is likely that the members of the convention knew little of him or his reputation. He certainly knew little of them. Twelve years abroad had insulated him from the realities of colonial politics on the ground. His speeches, and his scant writings, were of a high theoretical tone which would not have appealed to the pragmatic bourgeoisie of the Gold Coast. They were high achievers who aspired to take over the colonial state with a minimum of disruption to their lifestyle and status. But they needed a minion, an organizer to do the running about, and so they called on Nkrumah. In order to lure him from London they offered him a generous salary of £250 a year, which in the event they were unwilling to afford. One of their business supporters, Pa Grant, who may have known Nkrumah as a Catholic youth back in the village, sent the boat fare from Liverpool.

Before deciding to go to the Gold Coast, Nkrumah spoke to a British extramural lecturer from Oxford, Tony McLean, who had recently been out to investigate the prospect of setting up university-type courses in West Africa. McLean advised him that the proposed convention was a conservative caucus but that this did not preclude it from becoming a useful vehicle for raising consciousness in the sleepy doldrums of a small colony. The insularity of the colonial exiles in postwar Britain was such that, like the larger communities of European émigrés, they thrived in the hothouse of their own fantasies without any contact with political realities on the ground. Thus it was that Nkrumah, soon to become the most notable nationalist in all Africa, had to rely for sensitive political intelligence on a traveling white expatriate. In so doing he showed a broadness of mind, and an absence of racial prejudice, which remained consistent throughout his career. Though some of his freedom speeches were virulently hostile to British policies, many of his closest advisers continued to be British people, including in later years, his head of state, his commander-in-chief, his attorney-general, and his private secretary.

Once Nkrumah had decided to accept the invitation to return to the Gold Coast, and relinquish his long-cherished ambition to gain an academic doctorate, he used the sea voyage to gain an insight into African political realities as contrasted with the theories that flourished in the shadow of British communism. His first stop, Sierra Leone, was not the obvious model of a developing polity for a radical statesman to study. The country was even more sharply divided between the creolized élite and the rural mass than his own Gold Coast. In 1947, however, Nkrumah was not yet the populist par excellence, but a child of his time who assumed that the colonial élite would provide leadership towards self-government. Furthermore Nkrumah, the lone outsider, was constantly anxious to be accepted by association with the elder statesmen of Africa. More rationally, he also wanted to gain information about other West African countries since his idea of a union of West African states was firmly on his agenda. Return to the Gold Coast was thus further postponed while he tried to fraternize with the dark-suited aristocracy of Freetown in November 1947.

Nkrumah also broke his voyage in Liberia, the settler colony of former American slaves which had been given independence under a creole government exactly a century before. As a model for the Gold

Coast, Liberia was even more improbable than Sierra Leone. The illiterate population of the hinterland was wholly neglected by the ruling class, the country functioned on American currency rather than having its own bank, and the black bourgeoisie mimicked European styles of behavior strikingly alien in their symbolism. Yet Liberia was the one territory of West Africa that was politically — if not culturally or financially — independent and any union of West African states would need to accommodate the region's premier republic. Furthermore Liberia had begun to change, and President Tubman had been elected in 1944 with a mandate to loosen the domination of the Firestone Rubber Company and its plantations. But Nkrumah's stop in Liberia may have had rather more pragmatic and personal motives than the search for ideas and partners in the liberation struggle. Pragmatically Nkrumah hoped that by arriving on the Gold Coast as a deck passenger from Liberia he would attract less attention than he would as a student from Britain with a police file on his communist affiliation. More personally Nkrumah's visit to Liberia may have had to do with a search for his father's family.

One feature of his life which Nkrumah passes over in silence in his autobiography is the fact that his father was probably a Liberian. The family seems to have come from the borderless forest region of Liberia and the Ivory Coast which had for generations provided migrant workers to other regions of West Africa. When borrowing money to go to America Nkrumah had sought out the family diaspora in Lagos. The story of Nkrumah's father is not known, though mythology has cast him in every role from goldsmith to nightsoil porter. It is not surely established whether Nkrumah made contact with his father's family on his return. At some point he apparently visited the Ivory Coast, though it is not clear whether to forge links with neighboring politicians, despite his lack of spoken French, or more speculatively to visit a local shrine or to seek his paternal roots. Nkrumah's strong attachment to his mother remains the only documented certainty.

When Nkrumah finally reached the Gold Coast in December 1947 he did not hasten to Saltpond where the leaders were establishing the United Gold Coast Convention of which he was to become general secretary. He went instead to the gold-mining village of Tarkwa in the far west. After twelve years abroad he presumably wanted to take the temperature of the colony on familiar terrain and re-establish contact with people who remembered him. It was in Tarkwa that he met his mother and made his first speech on the familiar boards of a Catholic schoolroom. The old church network was probably more significant in determining his point of entry into Gold Coast society than the fact that Tarkwa was one of the few places in the country with a "proletarian" work-force of a kind potentially familiar to a quasi-communist political organizer. But "Kwame" Nkrumah probably only discovered a limited old-boy network created from his former lives as "Kofi" Nkrumah, the boy from Nzima who made good, or "Francis" Nkrumah, the teacher who had tried to follow in the steps of Dr. Aggrey, the scholar hero of the 1920s. His pupils would have been too few and too scattered to provide a hero's welcome or an hospitable base. In order to make his entrée onto the political stage Nkrumah was therefore dependent on his prospective employer, the Working Committee of the United Gold Coast Convention. After some delay he presented himself at Saltpond on 29 December 1947 and began work in an office rented, ironically if not subversively, from the United Africa Company, the premier commercial institution in the colony.

The United Gold Coast Convention

Although the United Gold Coast Convention was founded only in 1947 the roots of political experience among its lawyers, merchants, and graduate teachers went far deeper, as Dennis Austin, the outstanding historian of the period, explains in *Ghana Observed:*

> In 1947 this small independent professional and trading
> class could look back over more than fifty years of political
> effort, sometimes with, more often against the colonial ad-
> ministration. Educated at Mfantsipim or Adisadel College,
> or later at Achimota, taking their degrees at English univer-
> sities, they ran the newspapers sat on the Legislative Coun-
> cil, and criticized the government through political
> associations like the Aborigines' Rights Protection Society,
> the National Congress of British West Africa and local
> ratepayers' associations; they moved easily in English society
> without losing the awareness of their own African tradi-
> tions: indeed, they were among the first to defend them;
> but they had a liberal view of society — a lawyer's view, per-
> haps; they were never quite able to understand the appeal
> or techniques of mass organization; and they had a lawyer's
> caution, too, against rash, precipitate action.[1]

The rival to the lawyers' wing of the convention consisted of the chiefs. The relative importance of chiefs and intellectuals in the Gold Coast had fluctuated throughout the colonial period and was again to become a political issue during the early years of Nkrumah's ascendancy. The lawyers and the chiefs knew one another well and were often members of the same families, but their interests converged and diverged over time. The formalization of a British presence, after centuries of informal commercial administration, occurred on 6 March 1844 when a "bond" was signed between Great Britain and a confederacy of coastal chiefs. Thirty years later Britain curbed the southward influence of the Asante

Empire in a spectacular war and strengthened its own presence on the coast with a colonial constitution. An educated black élite gained the ascendancy until 1900 when, in the third stage of British penetration, local agents were replaced by white expatriates during the rampant heyday of imperialism. Gradually the cost of direct rule began to tell, and Africans emerged once more as the local agents of British policy. The lawyers at first saw this as a victory for themselves, but soon realized that the professional class was being bypassed by wealthy chiefs with rather different objectives. "Native authority" administrations were established in the 1920s and even Asante was allowed to rebuild its imperial administration in a modified and subservient form. Members of the intelligentsia served uneasily as officeholders in the councils of chiefs. The great African merchants were made even more anxious than the intellectuals by the rising power of the "aristocracy." They were even willing, by the 1940s, to put real money into organizing a political movement that would protect African commercial interests better than the great chiefs had done. Ironic though it may seem, it was the elderly, wealthy, timber merchant, Pa Grant, who found the £100 that were necessary to bring Nkrumah back to the Gold Coast from his left-wing student activities in Britain.

The most active leader of the new political Convention on the Gold Coast, and the man who sponsored Nkrumah's initiation into office, was Dr. J. B. Danquah. He was also the bridge between the chiefs, the lawyers, and the intellectuals. Danquah had royal connections but was also a barrister-at-law and held a doctorate in moral philosophy. Not only did he have links with all the factions in the convention, but he had also paved the way for Nkrumah. He had been the most innovative, even radical, member of the old guard. It was Danquah who had recognized that the future could not lie only with the tiny élite in the municipalities, nor with the aristocratic gerontocracy in the provinces, but needed to capture a broader swathe of society. Already he was looking to the youth whose time had not yet come but whose ambitions had been whetted by the growth of Western education. Danquah had begun to mobilize the "youngmen" as early as 1930 with a prescience that long preceded Nkrumah's own mobilizing activities. Danquah's early work with youth leagues, young men's associations, debating clubs, improvement societies, created a colony-wide youth conference which sought constitutional improvements. Danquah kept the youth movement in alliance with the chiefs and intellectuals when approaching a sympathetic governor, Sir Alan Burns, with demands for constitutional reform. In 1946 the "Burns Constitution" so changed the composition of the colonial legislative council that government officials and the representatives of the chambers of mines and of commerce were henceforth outnumbered by "unofficial" African appointees. This was radicalism indeed, but the times were moving much faster than the lawyers, and the great reform of 1946 was soon swept away. By 1948 the youth movements had found a new and more vocal hero in Kwame Nkrumah. The so-called "youngmen" swept Nkrumah along in a torrent of enthusiasm, leaving his mentor, Danquah, panting to keep up.

Nkrumah's service with the United Gold Coast Convention was very effective and within a year the eternal trouble-making student had become a famous nationalist leader. His charm, charisma, energy, rhetorical power, and organizing ability were single-mindedly devoted to building a broad coalition while avoiding making unnecessary enemies. Nkrumah's radicalism was always tempered with a liberal dash of caution, as in his long-running struggle to avoid a breach with the old leaders of the Convention. Received wisdom has it that Nkrumah fell out with Danquah almost immediately, though in fact neither was willing to relinquish the political advantages which the other might offer.

Nkrumah had the enthusiasm to breathe fire into a mass party while Danquah had the experience to avoid the snares along the road. Their symbiotic relationship of collaboration gradually turned to bitter competition and lasted for a decade to culminate in the 1960 election to choose the first executive president of an independent Republic of Ghana. Nkrumah won each round of the struggle and was the victor in the final election. His unpredicted successes need to be explained in all their complexity.

The World Context

Nkrumah began his Gold Coast career with such a string of coincidences in his favor that it is hard to judge how far his meteoric ascent was due to his own driving spirit and how far he simply happened to rise on the crest of the wave that was then sweeping the colonial world. The first factor to affect his opportunities was one which had nothing to do with the Gold Coast, or even with Africa, but occurred half a world away in India. This was the assassination of Gandhi. The death of Gandhi, and the sanctification of all that Gandhi had stood for, had a profound impact both on the pupil politicians of Africa and on their postwar masters in Europe. Nkrumah adopted the slogans of nonviolence both because he believed in them and because they were clearly a winning strategy in an age which had seen the defeat of the dictatorships and the reemergence of democracy throughout most of Western Europe. It became difficult for a colonial power to contemplate taking up arms against a movement which proclaimed both the democratic aims for which Europe had fought and the peaceful ideals for which Gandhi was martyred. Nkrumah and his followers made the most of these imperial inhibitions and wore white caps to proclaim their loyalty to the Indian ideal of freedom. When the colonial power was finally goaded into incarcerating African leaders, they reemerged with the letters P.G. for "prison graduate" emblazoned on their caps. The martyrdom of prison became almost a necessary qualification for high office in colonial Africa.

The success of Nkrumah owes something not only to events in India, but also to developments taking place in South Africa in 1948. The half-century of South African domination by Field Marshal Smuts and his collaborationist school of Afrikaner settlers willing to associate with British mining and manufacturing industries came to an abrupt and unexpected end in 1948. The "purified" white nationalists who wished to cut themselves off from the English-speaking middle class and seek better conditions for white peasants, pejoratively known as Boers, won a general election on a platform of extremist white-power policies. Rural and working-class white nationalists had partially missed out on South Africa's wartime prosperity and feared that English-speaking urban blacks would overtake them in economic opportunity and social status. Thus the assimilationist tradition of empire, which had made some progress, however haltingly, in segregationist South Africa, was terminated and a policy of *apartheid* or separation was launched. The new stance was morally repugnant to the mildly liberal political traditions in Britain, though industry continued to trade actively with South Africa and to benefit greatly from the South African gold mines, the profits of which were based on extreme forms of inequality and racial exploitation. British hostility to South African racism, however hypocritical, indirectly benefited the rival nationalists of West Africa with their very different black-led program. A condemnation of racism in South Africa and Rhodesia made it difficult to oppose demands for racial equality on the Gold Coast. Conversely the British commendation of black nationalism in West Africa, however ambivalent, had the unfortunate side-effect of accentuating the extremism of white nationalism in South Africa. In time the confrontation between the two ideologies came to dominate Africa's politics and become one of Nkrumah's major preoccupations. Before that, however, he still had to gain self-government at home. This required the mobilization of supporters in the diverse sectors of Gold Coast society.

Boycotts and Demonstrations

On the local Gold Coast scene one development which accidentally helped launch Nkrumah on his political path was the growing restiveness of working-class urban consumers who saw postwar wages being outstripped by postwar prices. The organizing of consumer protest took place not in Cape Coast or Saltpond where the old élite were establishing their Convention on the basis of traditional municipal politics, but in the newer eastern city of Accra. It was an Accra sub-chief who mobilized a protest movement in January 1948. It appears to be purely coincidence that this protest began within days of Nkrumah taking office as secretary to the Convention, but he was not slow in seeking to reap benefit from it. The Accra demonstrations were cleverly directed not only at the profiteers of big colonial trading companies but also at Lebanese and Syrian traders who, like any successful immigrants, were moneylenders as well as shopkeepers and were deemed a legitimate target for attack by both the professional class and the impoverished proletariat. Marches through Accra were noisy but had none of the personal violence of anti-Jewish marches in Europe or anti-Indian demonstrations in East Africa. They nevertheless put the nerves of the colonial administration on edge and provided a protest with coattails that a nationalist agitator could seize. They also stimulated a more radical form of agitation among war veterans trying to eke out a living on their service pensions.

The Gold Coast, like most colonies and dominions, had taken an active part in the Second World War. The economy was used to subsidize the siege economy of Britain and provide cocoa, gold, and vegetable oil for the war effort and postwar reconstruction. In addition

40,000 Gold Coast recruits had served overseas. These servicemen learned much in their travels. They discovered that white men and women performed menial tasks in other parts of the world and that skin color was an illegitimate source of status in the colonies. They learned about "equality of opportunity," which concept had caused members of the British armed forces to vote overwhelmingly for a socialist government and defeat Churchill the war-leader whom the ruling class had assumed to be such a popular hero. The colonial soldiers may also have realized that the war was being justified on a high moral tone of self-determination for peoples in Europe and Asia who had been undemocratically subjected to German and Japanese overlordship. The parallels were not lost on the demobilized soldiers of the Gold Coast when they returned home to poverty, unemployment, and racist domination. While the nationalists of Cape Coast discussed constitutional niceties, and the wage-earners of Accra boycotted foreign goods, some of the war veterans mobilized a protest against the indignity of winning a war only to become imperial paupers.

The demonstrations of 1948 found the Gold Coast colonial administration in disarray. White bureaucratic morale was low, pay was poor, staff was short, the central secretariat distrusted its own regional officers, and no one understood the changes affecting the world or the aspirations of Africans returning from abroad. Old-guard colonial officials with inflexible minds seem to have been out of touch with the times and it was they who were immediately responsible for what subsequently proved to be a momentous confrontation in February 1948. The ex-servicemen decided that if only they could present their case to the governor in person, in the fashion of loyal eighteenth-century protesters wishing to see their king, then all misunderstandings would be overcome. A march to the governor's castle-residence led to shooting. A few people were killed and injured. West Africa's erstwhile "model colony" witnessed a riot and business premises were looted. The African Revolution had begun.

When faced with disorder the local colonial administration reacted in classic British style. A minority of agitators, they felt, must be responsible for disturbing the peace. Sudden agitation could only be the work of wrongheaded men influenced by communists. The local agents of imperialism may have dimly anticipated that in a generation or two an élite cadre of blacks would be trained to take responsibility and mirror the paternalistic ideals of whites whose trusteeship they would eventually inherit. But in the heat of the moment they panicked. A cold war mentality seized them and "reds" were sought behind every disturbance. Since none could be found in a consumer boycott organized by a chief, nor in the march of loyal servicemen, the administration had to find communist agitators elsewhere. With a naïveté which almost defies belief they sought their scapegoats over in Saltpond among the professional elders of the Convention. They arrested six leaders, five of them conservative stalwarts and the sixth the newly hired party secretary, Kwame Nkrumah. Overnight Nkrumah and the "Big Six" became heroes and martyrs. They were initially taken away to Kumasi prison, but when it became clear that even in Asante sympathizers there were likely to attack the gaol in an attempt to free them, they were dispersed to individual prisons in the Northern Territories. After a few weeks the authorities began to recognize the scale of their blunder and the prisoners were released to be acclaimed as heroes.

Imperial Response

When the Gold Coast disturbances broke out Britain's Labour government was sunk in crisis and reluctantly had to turn its mind to colonial affairs. The colonial office in Attlee's reforming government was not predisposed to be radical over Africa. On the contrary the empire was

seen as necessary to further the two great policies of economic reconstruction at home and Soviet containment abroad. Policy was bluntly
expressed as the need to achieve "the most rapid development practi-
cable of our overseas possessions, since without such colonial development there can be no major improvement in the standard of living of
our own people at home." Nkrumah at his most radical could not have
been more succinct in explaining that the justification for imperialism
was the exploitation of colonial peoples for the benefit to the colonizer.
Nonsense about high-minded imperial trusteeship may have been
mouthed, but the reality was that Britain needed its empire. Any disturbance of the status quo, particularly one that might be linked to
communist agitators, was unwelcome. A disturbance on the relatively
wealthy Gold Coast was especially unwelcome. It did, however, won-
derfully focus the imperial mind on the broad postwar future.

The war of the 1940s in Europe had partly been about imperial
expansion. Germany had long envied Britain's dominant role in southern
Asia and planned to expand its own sphere of influence by conquering
the Soviet Union and taking a dominant role in northern Asia. The
Soviet Union retaliated, with British and American help, by restricting
German influence to Western Europe and creating an empire of its own
in central Europe both as a strategic buffer and as a zone of economic
extraction. The United States, which had also been a great imperial
power, conquering half of north America and gaining economic ascendancy over South America, now expanded its neo-imperial influence to
eastern Asia and western Europe. The old colonial superpowers, France
and Britain, were left with the dilemma of how to retain their role in the
world. In Southeast Asia France surrendered its territories gracelessly to
America but went on to fight for control of its settler territories in North
Africa. Britain, by contrast, decided to hand the administration of its
colonial territories to local politicians. Nationalism was a continuation

of imperialism by other and more efficient means, claimed Ronald Robinson, the historian of empire. Despite the traumas over the partitions of India and Palestine, and despite the ensuing conflicts and massacres of 1948, Britain expected to find client politicians in the new imperial territories who would work for Britain as effectively as those in the old white dominions had done. There was, however, still some hesitation about how to deal with Africa.

The broad if unspoken assumption that emerged during 1948 was that Africa was to be seen as two separate spheres of policy. In eastern Africa the development of a thinly peopled region would be associated with white settlement of the Kenyan and Rhodesian type backed up by government projects such as the Tanganyika groundnut scheme. In West Africa, by contrast, the future would depend on the training of a local élite capable of taking responsibility. Any alternative strategy, it was feared, might play into the hands of Soviet imperialists who would seek a place in the African sun by sponsoring unacceptable black zealots. Nationalists could only be tolerated if they were willing to co-operate with Britain to the exclusion of any dealings with Russia or America. The threat of American imperialism was still only dimly perceived though one of the objectives of the new Empire-Commonwealth was to help close the "dollar gap," as the balance of payments deficit was then called, by channeling colonial produce through the London commodity markets to the advantage of Britain. It was against this background that a "new deal" in Africa, envisaged since the war years, was unwittingly set in motion by the Accra "riot" of February 1948. The decisions taken in the heat of the moment proved to be irreversible.

The New Politics
It became clear within days that the Gold Coast administration had committed a grave error by arresting the leaders of the United Gold

Coast Convention. Firstly they had alienated the sober conservatives who would have been their natural allies in an untroubled and gradual transfer of power. Worse still, they had created a new leader whose message was more urgent. Nkrumah emerged from prison to begin his campaign for "self-government now." Overnight he had become a popular hero. Neither the white administration nor the black bourgeoisie were comfortable with his intemperate haste. The black gradualists, however, could not afford to seem lukewarm, and the administration had shot itself in the foot, so that Nkrumah was free to make the running. He began to experiment with ideas of political organization.

Nkrumah's initial ideas about organization were an odd amalgam of contemporary thinking which he would have preferred not to publicize. Although he had been fortunate to be arrested and given the martyr's crown, he was unlucky that his private papers fell into the hands of the police. Police attempts to discredit him as a communist were somewhat wide of the mark. The former Catholic and admirer of the Fabians described himself as a "Marxist socialist" and as a "nondenominational Christian." His early thoughts about political organization seem to have had a subversive tinge and ran more on the lines of a secret association than of a mass party. While in America Nkrumah had apparently enrolled in a student fraternity whose ideals were different from Christianity or socialism and whose members swore binding loyalty to each other rather than to society at large. It was perhaps not surprising that a lone and insecure student should have sought close acceptance by peers. But the insecurity lasted into later life and Nkrumah's need for admiration caused him to hold tightly to his friends but behave harshly towards his critics. This student experience of seeking solidarity in closed groups also led Nkrumah to think in similar terms in Africa. When he was arrested, on 12 March 1948, a proposal was found among his private papers for the establishment of a secret lodge called "the Circle."

The blueprint that Nkrumah had uncharacteristically committed to paper was a forthright call for a revolutionary vanguard. Service, sacrifice, and suffering were to be the hallmarks of membership. The first aim was a united states of West Africa, the naïve ideal of the exiles who had nurtured Nkrumah rather than the objective of the territorial nationalists for whom he worked. The ultimate aim was a union of African socialist republics. Detractors in the colonial administration invariably added the word "Soviet" to the proposal in an effort to prove the subversive intent of the Circle. The Circle was designed to be authoritarian in order to control the masses and prevent them from falling under the sway of "demagogues, quislings and traitors." Members would swear an unbreakable oath of loyalty to each other and would accept the unconditional leadership of Nkrumah. In addition to oathtaking as the cement of the organization, all members would meditate on the twenty-first day of each month and observe a fast from sunrise to sunset. Cells were to meet monthly and the grand council annually. All affairs of the Circle were to be secret and would never be communicated by post or telephone. It was perhaps not surprising that Nkrumah was later referred to by the governor as "our local Hitler."

Nkrumah's thinking about political organization is interesting for the question it raises of the affiliation of nationalist leaders to ritualized international movements such as the freemasons. Freemasonry itself had broad local roots and became strong in independent Ghana. It provided a bond of "loyalty" among the professional classes, especially the legal fraternity, which was so exclusive as to vitiate the rule of law and eventually caused freemasonry to be outlawed. In francophone West Africa freemasonry spread among the top political echelons and state presidents became grandmasters of their national lodges. This cemented their personal links with masons among the ruling élite of France but cut them off from fellow leaders in the rest of Africa. Nkrumah's path proved, in the event, to be a different one. He turned to "the people" to create a mass movement rather than to the "vanguard" to organize subversive secret cells. His true genius lay in inspired oratory and not in Machiavellian plotting. His background of poverty on the margins of the Gold Coast gave him more credibility as a populist leader than all his overseas education.

Youth Movement

The loudest and most visible of the followers that Nkrumah recruited into politics on behalf of the Convention, and later into his own People's Party, were the young men whom Danquah had already identified as being the key to the future. The core of Nkrumah's youth movement was made up of people whom the middle class dubbed the "verandah boys." They were school-leavers and dropouts with varying levels of unfinished education who came to town in search of paid employment and slept rough on the back verandahs of distant relatives. These detached youths, who had escaped from agricultural drudgery to bring their poor skills and high aspirations to town, were the ideal recipients for Nkrumah's first message, Africa for the Africans. The wider ideal of West African unity was put on the back burner and the speeches concentrated on the opportunities that would be available once the people were free. Nkrumah's couriers carried a radical message of "Free-Dom" back to the villages. Old hymn tunes were adapted to new songs of liberation which welcomed traveling orators, and especially Nkrumah himself, to mass rallies throughout the Gold Coast.

At first the Convention elders were enthusiastic about the success of their secretary. The old timber merchant, Pa Grant, continued to finance the organization and to welcome the new politics which diminished the influence of his rivals, the chiefs. Danquah assured the Convention that Nkrumah would not let them down, though other leaders began to fear his high profile and his radical rhetoric. Gradually the success of the hired worker came to be seen as a challenge and the Convention contemplated dropping him. They only feared to do so lest they lose the youth constituency. Tension rose until a temporary compromise was sought in mid-1949 by switching Nkrumah from the post of general secretary to that of honorary treasurer. This was a curious appointment, especially since one of Nkrumah's avowed weaknesses was a lack of any understanding of finance, and it did not solve the underlying ideological rift that had opened up. Eventually Nkrumah broke with the Convention in 1949 to turn his youth movement into an autonomous "people's party." In an attempt to retain a broader base and credible roots, the new party was firmly linked to the ideals of the Convention and named the CPP or Convention People's Party.

Cocoa Farmers

The enthusiasm of undereducated youngsters was not enough to create a party of substance which could both command the attention of the colonial authorities and gain a broad base of support among voters. In order to be taken seriously Nkrumah needed to find a more sober set of constituents, and preferably one with financial assets which could be invested in the costly business of disseminating propaganda. Once again he was fortunate in his timing and found an issue of burning topicality among the cocoa farmers who provided the backbone of the country's wealth. Indeed, cocoa was important not only to the Gold Coast, but also to Britain, which sold half of it abroad for dollars. By recruiting support among the cocoa farmers, who produced no less than two-thirds of the world's cocoa, Nkrumah once again entered the imperial limelight. He threatened the semi-enlightened self-interest of Britain's rulers.

The cocoa factor made the politics of the Gold Coast different from those of any other colony in Africa. Before 1900 the main cocoa grower in West Africa had been the plantation island of São Tomé where cocoa was grown, fermented, and dried on Portuguese factory estates worked by quasi-slave labor from Angola. On the Gold Coast the British discovered that climatic conditions made it possible for cocoa to be sun dried after being more cheaply grown by African farmers without colonial capital or costly management. The cocoa manufacturers incidentally gained moral credit for boycotting "slavegrown" Portuguese cocoa. The coastal peasant industry grew rapidly and spread into parts of Asante. Some farmers became substantial black entrepreneurs and hired migrant workers from the north and from the French colonies. Cocoa trees, however, suffered from a serious disease called swollen shoot. The colonial agriculture department advised, correctly, that the only way of preventing a disastrous spread of the infection was to cut down and burn all diseased trees. This may have protected the colonial economy as a whole from further ravages, but for individual farmers the recipe was catastrophic. By early in 1948 the farmers, their employees, and the provincial market towns of the cocoa belt were in vigorous confrontation with the colonial administration. It was a situation ripe for a political organizer to pluck ready-made from the tree.

Nkrumah soon discovered how to win credit for organizing the cocoa protests. Farmers were quite ready to believe that government was trying to rob them of the buoyant new cocoa prices. Indeed, throughout the war government had robbed the farmers by paying low prices to producers and investing the colonial surpluses in Europe rather than in Africa. Government interference, moreover, was not new and protests against agricultural ordinances were the standard fare of colonial rebellion. Elsewhere in Africa the compulsory growing of peasant cotton, the requirement to terrace land against erosion, the order to plant cassava as a famine crop, the forced selling of rice, had all caused great uprisings of rural peoples. Now the hitherto rather prosperous Gold Coast farmers, who had shown some skill in withholding harvests to push up prices during the great depression, were on the receiving end of an unpopular government order. Protest was mobilized among landowners and normally conservative rural districts were unexpectedly radicalized. More strikingly still, some chiefs, who previously feared that the politics of protest might unleash revolution, were so threatened by the crisis of swollen shoot disease that they entered into confrontation with the government in alliance with the young radicals set to work by Nkrumah.

Women and Liberation

While British colonial thinkers were planning their responses to the African awakening, Nkrumah was seeking ways of broadening his political base yet further. The liberation movements of Africa discovered that one way of mobilizing support was to seek the approval of women. When men were compulsorily recruited to labor in chain gangs, to dig underground, to serve as carriers, to weed the plantations, to join overseas military regiments, women were left with heavy burdens of responsibility as farmers and farm laborers, as wage earners and heads of household, as load bearers and urban traders. Responsibility for the domestic economy of both town and countryside turned some Gold Coast women into unusually successful businesswomen. They enhanced their commercial acumen and diversified into the colony's entrepreneurial and transport sectors. The support of powerful market women became important to Nkrumah as they were able to fund some of his early organizing ventures. The decision by the British Empire to give votes to women when democracy was devolved was almost as dramatic as giving votes to non-property owners and non-literates. In

Europe votes for women had only recently spread to France and were still not universal elsewhere. In Africa universal franchise encouraged Nkrumah to pioneer experiments in mobilizing women's power. The ideology that women are equal, that women held up half the sky as the Chinese would have it, was not easy to get across. Central decision-making remained in male hands and women's power was insulated in special-purpose women's organizations, a tradition which was to carry on throughout the African Revolution even in countries where women actively supported an armed struggle against settlers. In 1948 Gold Coast women were cheerleaders, fund-raisers, street-demonstrators, boycott organizers, but were not members of central committees where male domination remained virtually as exclusive as in Britain.

The Proletariat
In 1948 it might have been expected that one source of support for the new politics would be the trade union movement. Though wage-earning was but a small sector of the Gold Coast economy, the old railway town of Sekondi nonetheless had a significant proletarian labor force. This, and the adjacent 1920s' "new town" built around the port of Takoradi, was also the main area of industrial production with 90 percent of the Gold Coast's manufacturing wage-earners. The railway workers had the oldest and strongest trade union movement in the mini-conurbation. They had begun to unionize in the 1920s and were capable of sustaining strikes of several weeks in demand of shorter working hours, better housing conditions and, above all, improved wages. In a colonial society in which wage employment was predominantly in state-owned enterprises, the union movement was mainly directed against government and so had a potential affinity to any opposition movement. The railway workers seemed natural allies to Nkrumah in his search for a wide-ranging coalition to challenge the

local colonial authorities. They were far removed in the social spectrum from the intellectuals and lawyers of Cape Coast, but Nkrumah's breakaway nationalist movement was wholly eclectic in its search for allies. Nkrumah, moreover, had at least some limited experience of the aspirations of the wage-earning classes from his occasional contacts with the black proletariat in postwar Britain. Nkrumah's accommodation with the trade unions was to be short-lived but was nonetheless useful to his credibility when he was negotiating with a British cabinet containing senior trade union members. A much wider constituency needed to be awakened, however, if he was to gain majority backing in the colony.

Political Geography

In 1948 the Gold Coast may have been the "model colony," and may have been advanced by the economic and educational standards of most other British colonies in Africa, let alone French or Portuguese ones. The level of economic extraction was high and the gross national product compared favorably with that of the poorer regions of southern Europe. But the proportion of cocoa's value that was taken as local revenue and invested in infrastructure and social services was small, and the country was more backward than its wealth warranted. Two railways had been built between the coast and Asante, one to meet strategic and mining requirements and the other to extract cocoa and timber. No direct road or rail linked the administrative capital to the other coastal towns before the Nkrumah nationalists gained power and gave communications a new priority. Likewise few of the road surfaces were tarred under the colonial administration, though it must not be forgotten that at the time all-weather trunk roads were still rare in the Soviet Union, or even in parts of the United States, let alone in Africa. Nkrumah spent many of his early months in Africa coated in choking dust as he hitchhiked up and down the colony forging links between small, widely scattered communities. The basic unit of transport was the wooden "mammy lorry" built on a Bedford chassis and designed to carry cocoa, root crops, and passengers. Rivers were perilously crossed on small hand-drawn ferries anchored to cables. Even the Volta River was not bridged until Nkrumah embarked on his great public works program in the 1950s. Local supplies of electricity lit a few towns and mines, but elsewhere firewood, charcoal, and kerosene were the basis of cooking, lighting, and occasionally refrigeration in wayside bars. Telephone wires on rudimentary poles reached district commissioners at the ends of muddy laterite roads.

Social Environment

The social integration of the Gold Coast territories was rather greater than might have been expected from their historic fragmentation and economic isolation. The links gave Nkrumah the opportunity to contemplate a "national" scale of political mobilization across all four Gold Coast territories. This prospective unification was later challenged by his rivals but the colonial legacy gave him an advantage over the ethnic and regional appeals of his opponents. The use of English as the language of wider communication was particularly important. A pidgin form of English had more or less replaced Portuguese as the trade language of the south from the seventeenth century. Standard English was the language of justice, administration, and education, though primary schools and church missions preferred the use of local vernaculars for quicker results. Only when Nkrumah gained power did he insist that English be adopted nationwide as the language of first schooling. Education had been the key to social change on the Gold Coast but it had grown slowly and patchily to meet perceived colonial needs at minimum cost. In the 1920s Guggisberg, the down-to-earth governor upon whom many of the later nationalist politicians tacitly modeled their public works policies, actually restricted the availability of education in order to finance his élite secondary school at Achimota. This aspect of modernizing policy was less appealing to the populist side of Nkrumah than Guggisberg's decisions to build a major hospital, an artificial port, and a new railway. In the 1930s, when Nkrumah was still a schoolteacher, the country had four million people but less than 75,000 children were in primary school; the great majority were in the south, in areas of Catholic, Methodist, and Presbyterian mission influence. Not only was education restricted in its availability but criticism was regularly leveled at the schools for failing to provide technical education, though technical education did not lead very far in a country without industry. Pupils preferred academic schooling leading, they hoped, to white collar jobs with white collar salaries. When jobs and salaries failed to materialize they were only too ready to follow Nkrumah.

In one respect school education alienated children from the traditional values and customs of their society and tried to mold them into black Britons with empire loyalties and school caps. In the opposite direction it created a united stratum of school-leavers who identified with the Gold Coast, rather than with any one ethnic or regional section of it. Education therefore unwittingly and ironically kindled a hotbed of nationalism in which the seeds of independence germinated. School-leavers escaping from rural underemployment drifted to the towns seeking higher social status and often faced long periods of unemployment with time to dream about a political future of unlimited opportunity. A few gained access to the ladder of social mobility, but the rest were ideal recruits for a populist preacher who proclaimed "Seek ye first the political kingdom" and assured them that all else would then be added unto them.

At the other end of the educational spectrum from the school dropouts who became Nkrumah's loudest supporters a different development occurred in 1948 with far-reaching consequences. This was the establishment of a university on the site of the old teacher training college at Achimota. The idea of higher education for Africans was little short of revolutionary except in one college in Sierra Leone. None of the other powers contemplated college education in Africa, and no universities were proposed for the settler colonies. The first modern degree courses in Africa were established where African leadership was expected to take responsibility within a generation or so, in Uganda, in Nigeria, and on the Gold Coast. The proposals were modest, entry was at the old matriculation level, and the first tiny batches of graduates did not emerge for several years. But universities rapidly became the symbol of African emancipation, the proof of political maturity. Even Nkrumah, the egalitarian champion of the *sans-culottes,* was seduced by the prestige of a university and allowed it to evolve on patterns of almost medieval ceremonial and of Cambridge élitism. The emerging graduates, with degrees in classics and chemistry rather than civil engineering and public hygiene, were to be Nkrumah's most highly trained civil servants. They also became his most articulate critics, though few of them developed a sensitive political touch, as the governments of the 1970s were painfully to demonstrate.

Constitutional Change

Britain readily recognized that constitutional change could not await the training of a cohort of graduates to manage the affairs of the Gold Coast. The inquiry into the Accra riots, which had so unexpectedly thrown this quiet backwater into turmoil, shrewdly suggested that the best solution was to devise a new constitution in which Africans were made to bear more responsibility for policy choices and in which blame for failure could be less squarely placed at the door of the British. The constitutional proposals were drawn up by a commission of middle-class Africans trusted not to develop anything that might allow the colony to escape from British tutelage along unexpectedly radical routes. The debate reverted to the old conflict between the intelligentsia and the chiefs, which had been temporarily bridged by Danquah and the Convention. This time the chiefs, whom governors had hitherto preferred to the more eloquent municipal property-owners, were turned down and their claim to an upper house in a proposed legislative assembly was rejected. Men of education and property were expected to control the new parliament on behalf of commoners, and chiefs were to be given reserved seats in a single chamber.

Nkrumah was caught in a cleft stick by the new constitution. His immediate reaction was to reject it as a fraudulent attempt by the British to postpone self-government, or to hand power to the propertied class rather than to the "people." His second reaction was to work within the constitution and attempt to use it to win power for the masses. It was his great achievement to succeed in doing both. By denouncing the constitution as a fraud he gained huge popularity among the disparate factions of aggrieved people who supported his radical enthusiasm. Simultaneously he worked within the constitution to create one of the most successful political parties that was ever built in Africa.

The constitutional proposals of the Coussey Commission were presented in October 1949 and Nkrumah, as a good politician, immediately called together a broad "People's Assembly" in which to test the temperature of the colony by listening to debates on the constitutional question. The assembly was composed not only of party members but also of youth organizations, trade unions, farmers' representatives, and ex-servicemen. They expressed a preference for a franchise without property qualifications, a separate house of chiefs rather than reserved seats for chiefs in a single chamber, a responsible cabinet in which only the minister for defense would be nominated by Whitehall, and immediate self-governing dominion status under the Statute of Westminster.

The assembly's suggested amendments to the constitutional proposals were rejected by the colonial administration. Nkrumah tried to negotiate a compromise with the governor, but his political machine had been tuned up to embark on a campaign of "Positive Action" in demand of immediate self-government. Positive action meant civil disobedience, non-cooperation, boycotts, and strikes designed to disrupt the country without resort to violence. The alternative to positive action, termed "Tactical Action" or negotiation, would have been Nkrumah's preferred strategy, but the Accra crowd wanted more urgency.

On 8 January 1950 Nkrumah announced that Positive Action was to begin at midnight. Within a fortnight he was arrested and condemned to three years in prison. The chiefs and the intelligentsia assumed, in Danquah's words, that the "wolf had been driven away" and they got down to disputing with each other over the political inheritance. They had seriously misjudged the situation, and the common people flocked to enroll in the Convention People's Party to claim their national birthright. Colonial officials now recognized more readily than the old political leaders that a Nkrumah government had to be among the possible political options.

Election Victory

In 1951, while Nkrumah was in gaol, Britain organized in the Gold Coast the first general election ever to be held in Africa under universal franchise. The Convention People's Party organized itself to bring victory to its absent leader. The single most important factor in Nkrumah's rise to power was probably his use of the press. Radio was of limited availability in the years before transistors, and broadcasting was a monopoly of colonial government anyway. But newspapers, however crude, could be published and disseminated. The Gold Coast had a sufficiently broad base of literate school-leavers for printed messages to reach the whole country and be read to meetings in church halls and to gatherings under village trees. The CPP press became strident in the extreme and stern efforts were made by the administration to curtail its slanders and curb its journalists. The biggest headlines were devoted to Nkrumah's slogans demanding self-government now. In the end the colonial government had decided that the only way to stop Nkrumah's campaign was to arrest him for sedition. Once again the authorities had handed him a political advantage second to none by casting him in the role of symbolic victim of all oppression. Each and every man and woman in the Gold Coast could transpose his or her grievance, whatever it might be, to the imprisoned Nkrumah.

Nkrumah's lieutenants organized an election campaign on his behalf. The platform was simple and unambiguous: Free-Dom. The old Convention leaders mounted a rival campaign with a multi-syllabic manifesto full of subtleties that cut little ice with a broad electorate. Nkrumah's aides, led by K. A. Gbedemah, proved entirely competent to organize a general election strictly according to the British rulebook. From behind bars Nkrumah provided even more effective inspiration than if he had been in charge. In goal he was unable to harm his own cause by rash petulance or subversion. The campaign was hugely colorful as great crowds sang the nationalist hymns. The voting was quite unambiguous. Nkrumah and the CPP won the first general election in colonial Africa by a landslide.

2

Government Leader

Nkrumah stepped onto the world stage at 1:00 P.M. on 12 February 1951. There are two stories about his release from prison after the famous electoral victory of his party. Nkrumah's own story, believed by himself and by most of his biographers, is that he emerged from prison to a hero's welcome. This received wisdom says that a huge crowd had gathered outside the prison to welcome him and carry him shoulder high. His faithful lieutenant, Gbedemah, was on hand to lead him through the sea of upturned faces. A two-hour progress by open car through the jubilant mass led to the Accra arena where a sheep was sacrificed to cleanse the leader's feet after the contamination of prison. No general, said Nkrumah, could have felt more proud of his army and no soldiers could have shown greater affection for their leader.

The second story about Nkrumah's release is that of the governor who released him. According to this version the governor was keenly anxious to avoid the kind of stage-managed heroics that Nkrumah's autobiography describes. The decision to release Nkrumah from prison was a difficult one, and one which the governor alone took, though probably in the full awareness that he might be fatefully influencing the course of imperial history. He decided that no prior news of his decision should leak out and that Nkrumah should be released without warning or announcement. So, says the governor's version, when Nkrumah stepped out of James Fort into the sunlight he found himself alone in an empty street.

The authority for both versions of the story is actually one and the same person. Erica Powell became private secretary to the governor soon after self-government was granted to the Gold Coast and it was the governor himself who told her of the difficulty of his decision to release Nkrumah and of his success in stage-managing the event so that there would be no unseemly celebration of the nationalist success. He sincerely believed his own version of the event. Erica Powell subsequently became private secretary to Nkrumah, by then prime minister, and she was responsible for writing his autobiography to mark the independence of Ghana. It was therefore she who wrote the account of the crowd scenes which acclaimed him at the prison gate. He was perfectly convinced that news of his release had been leaked and that crowd jubilation made 12 February 1951 the greatest day of his life. Such incompatible but influential memories are the stuff of history, as the faithful secretarial chronicler made clear without passing judgment.

In 1951 Nkrumah faced three tasks. The first was to learn the art of government. The second was to create a nation out of the four territories that were loosely joined together as the Gold Coast. The third was to win independence. All three required ingenuity, drive, and compromise. All three led to sharp competition between the People's Party and its more conservative rivals. In all three Nkrumah was so successful that within nine years he had become the executive president of a unified nation with complete political freedom. He co-operated closely with the colonial civil service who were sometimes his opponents, but were also his tutors. He strengthened his nationwide party to defeat the forces of separatism and devolution which were launched against him. And finally he persuaded Britain that it had no alternative but to cooperate with his program and grant Ghana independence as a Commonwealth republic after relatively short periods of internal self-government and of dominion status under the Crown.

Sir Charles Arden-Clarke

The governor who decided to release Nkrumah from gaol and appoint him Leader of Government Business in the new parliamentary assembly was Sir Charles Arden-Clarke. Arden-Clarke's thoughts on the future of the British Empire in Africa had evolved during a recent tour of duty in Asia. While stationed on the remote north coast of Borneo he occasionally shared a sundowner with another lonely proconsul out in the Far East. This was Malcolm Macdonald, son of Britain's first Labour Prime Minister, a former secretary of state for the colonies and now governor-general of Southeast Asia responsible for holding the territories recovered from Japan and resisting the advances of communism in Asia. Together they peered down the road to African emancipation along which successive Labour and Conservative governments were inexorably drawn. To some real degree they were responsible for preparing the map.

Arden-Clarke arrived on the Gold Coast in August 1949 with three major strengths to his career. In Southeast Asia he had witnessed the rise of communism and the organization of terrorism. This experience was to be invaluable to him in assessing, and rejecting, the information and advice that were presented to him when he arrived in West Africa. Local administrators on the Gold Coast thought that they were the victims of violent plots, of communist conspiracies, and that stern measures would have to be taken to suppress the emergent nationalist forces of West Africa. Arden-Clarke, with his Asian experience, took a much more relaxed view of African nationalism and very soon saw in it the seeds of conservatism that were to lead nationalists to become ideal partners in Commonwealth development. This assessment arose partly from the new governor's second strength which was his experience in Bechuanaland where he had been sent as resident commissioner at a time when the ruling regent, Tshekedi Khama, was in violent confrontation with the British authorities. Arden-Clarke turned the situation round so skillfully that he and Tshekedi became close collaborators with mutual respect if not friendship. This skill in finding the best in people and working with them was to be the basis of Arden-Clarke's genius as the father of the new colonialism in Africa.

The third of Arden-Clarke's strengths was the experience he had acquired in northern Nigeria in the inter-war period where he gained a familiarity with the pomp and circumstance of African politics. His ability to adopt theatrical roles, to attend endless durbars and ceremonies, to treat chiefs with gravitas, to enhance people's self-respect with receptions and dinner parties, served him well. He broke down the traditional barriers of racial exclusivity and created an integrated élite of nationalists and expatriates. Arden-Clarke was described as a man of steel, but he actually liked Africa, and genuinely wanted Africans to gain some of the benefits from the new imperialism which he was pioneering on behalf of the government of Great Britain. His role in Africa can legitimately be compared to that of Mountbatten who had masterminded the transfer of power in India.

The Art of Government

Learning the art of government was the first difficult task which Nkrumah faced in 1951, but it was also the one in which he received the broadest degree of cooperation. When Arden-Clarke released him from gaol he simultaneously decided to groom him as his agent for the development of semi-responsible government. The civil service was briefed accordingly. Old racial and ideological prejudices were suppressed, and full cooperation was accorded to the new politicians. The white establishment might complain in private about the idiosyncrasies of their new administrative partners, but in public all support was given to Nkrumah's men. The governor privately called in the three expatriate members of the government and told them that they could use all their powers of persuasion in the executive council to influence policy, but that they would never use their vote to oppose the elected majority. Responsible government was to be responsible government with the freedom to make bad choices as well as good ones. On the visible surface, at least, politicians were in charge.

In practice there were limits to Nkrumah's power in 1951. His position was that of "leader of government business," not chief minister as became the norm in colonies which later followed the Ghana path to self-government. The chairman of the cabinet was the governor and three important ministerial portfolios were reserved for officials. The authority of African ministers was also limited by the influence of their permanent secretaries who, although quite unfamiliar with parliamentary practice, had long experience of administrative questions. The new cabinet was taken aback in 1951 to find that the civil service had already drawn up the budget and that they had little opportunity to interfere with its content. The dominant role of the civil service was a quintessential part of the British system of government and was to remain an entrenched heritage of Ghana. But the taming of the politicians, and the educating of the bureaucrats, proceeded so smoothly under the benign eye of Arden-Clarke that within a year the procedures were accelerated for the transfer of more responsibility.

In 1952 the governor withdrew from the chairmanship of the cabinet and appointed Nkrumah as his prime minister. The governor's seat in cabinet was transferred to a deputy governor. Parliamentary business proceeded smoothly and the conduct of debates was supervised by an African speaker elected by the House. The governor, in imitation of the new British queen, opened parliament with a speech from the throne on the general outlines of the policy that his prime minister proposed to follow. The official white civil servants in cabinet were replaced by elected black ministers. Even the ministry of finance was brought into the political arena and given to Gbedemah. Although the governor half-humorously remembered these years as ones of perpetual crisis, the path towards self-government seemed straight and free from difficulties.

Learning about political management was comparatively easy in the early 1950s because of the favorable economic conditions in the country. The price of cocoa, like that of other world commodities, rose sharply during the Korean war and enabled the new government to spend freely. One great success was the social welfare and community development program. Nkrumah's experience of Fabian socialism caused him to lay great stress on the creation of a welfare state and the provision of tap water to the villages and of concrete drains for town latrines. Community programs and school development, however much they were inherited from the colonial agenda, were visible and popular signs of a new government at work. Even more dramatic was the new program of road-building which enabled people to travel more freely and farm produce to be carried more cheaply. The Gold Coast was crowded with enthusiastic people on the move, both geographically and socially. In all the bustle the People's Party enhanced its popularity by showing that self-government was more than hot rhetoric. Policies may have been devised by officials briefed to implement welfare colonialism, but the credit was garnered by Nkrumah.

The availability of money in the fat years presented trainee ministers with problems as well as opportunities. One question that they faced concerned their own personal standard of living. Should they accept brick houses and motor cars as part of the perks of office and how could such extravagance be squared with the egalitarian principles of socialist "men of the people"? More serious still were the temptations to divert government money to local ends. Crises arose when middle-ranking politicians were charged with the unlawful use of public funds. The first confusions involved the indiscriminate mixing of party and government interests, a problem not unfamiliar in British politics but somehow deemed heinously immoral in Africa. Official money was apparently channeled into party coffers by those who could not distinguish between the two facets of a corporate common concern. More seriously still, private benefits occasionally began to be creamed off public assets.

Bribery and embezzlement were not a large-scale problem in the self-governing Gold Coast but they were a creeping disease that came to affect not only Ghana but more especially other newly emancipated countries in Africa. The transition from being the opposition to colonial government to being the agent of colonial government was difficult. Some nationalist hotheads in other colonies had seen embezzlement almost as a patriotic duty. Embracing the transition to vigilance in protecting the state coffers and prudence in spending tax revenues now required a strenuous rethinking of loyalties. It was perhaps one of Nkrumah's misfortunes that he was the first African leader to face the difficult moral dilemmas that choosing one's loyalties entailed in the colonial transition. Critical observers had little understanding of the pressures involved and not much awareness of the history of corruption in their own societies.

Public men and women in Africa were subject to concentric circles of pressure radiating out into society. The first loyalty which they were called upon to honor was loyalty to the extended family. Finding school-places, salaried jobs, business loans, import licenses, for the far-ranging network of relatives that helped each politician to win a top position was a debt of gratitude and responsibility that had to be honored. Next in line came the local community which had to be offered the tangible benefits of roads and clinics and bus stations. Beyond that were the expectations of all those with a fellow-feeling for the new "big men" because they shared a common language and ethnic identity. Only last in the line of loyal debts could a politician see the public good, society at large, and the nation-state which Nkrumah-the-leader so firmly had in his own sights.

Even more delicate than the control of state money was the control of resources belonging to quasi-governmental organizations. The first of these to become a political issue was the Cocoa Purchasing Company. This company was set up with party encouragement to buy cocoa for the national marketing board in competition with private brokers. It aimed to encourage the industry by using its profits to advance loans to growers for farm improvements. It soon ran into trouble by giving favorable consideration to party members, and even allowing its resources to be used for party purposes. Worse still the controlling of the new company's finances, and the auditing of its books, required a degree of skill and probity which was difficult to inculcate in a new generation of white-collar workers. Corruption came to be suspected in the affairs of the company and accusations reached into the higher levels of the party. Controlling the finances of state-owned enterprises to ensure that they were managed in the public interest became an increasingly difficult challenge to the successive Nkrumah administrations.

Development

The first Nkrumah government was able partly to finance its ambitious development programs out of financial reserves which had hitherto been in London, and used to strengthen the pound sterling, rather than be locally invested in development projects in Africa. The postwar colonial administration had planned to spend a million pounds a year on "development." Once Nkrumah had access to the national funds he proposed to spend ten million a year and actually spent rather more. In 1951 such an ambitious spending program could be launched in all probity. It did, however, create a pattern of expectations for the future which it would be difficult to meet. So long as current cocoa prices remained high, the farmers could be kept content while still allowing a margin of cocoa profit for government. But when the reserves began to run out and the price of cocoa began to fall, the easy years of managing the boom gave way to the harsh years of confronting the recession. Nkrumah himself had great difficulty in coming to terms with the relatively limited real resources of his country when the heady days of high prices and long-accumulated overseas reserves were ended.

One of the biggest sources of expenditure in the first flush of nationalist enthusiasm was the rapid expansion of the senior civil service. Part of this expansion was achieved by bringing in more expatriates to staff education, public works, administration, planning, and welfare. The number of expatriate senior officers rose from five hundred to fifteen hundred. Foreign employees in both the private sector and the public sector increased even after independence. Well-paid employment in the colonies for professionally qualified Britons, and even some not so well qualified, was seen as economically desirable in Britain.

An even more spectacular feature of growth than the rising tide of expatriates was the Africanization of the expanding senior civil service. The two-hundred-odd senior African civil servants whom Nkrumah found in post had increased to nearly one thousand by the end of his first term. This African expansion was a powerful engine of growth but also a powerful moderating influence on the early radicalism of the People's Party. Nkrumah had soon learned to live with the colonial civil service knowing that in the event of confrontation expatriates would concede to politicians or in extreme cases could be retired to Britain. In the case of the rapidly growing black bureaucracy he was dealing with a class that he would have to learn to accommodate permanently. In the early years, however, well-paid government employees were among Nkrumah's most important supporters and the prospect of the bureaucracy as an enemy of the party was but a small cloud in a serene sky. Self-government was smooth, peaceful, and expansionist. Independence was deemed to be just over the horizon.

The Independence Election

Plans were made for a general election in 1954 to test the popularity of the Nkrumah brand of nationalism and open the way to the transfer of power. The Nkrumah independence constitution provided for adult suffrage by men and women over the age of twenty-one in 104 single-member constituencies. Faint-hearted expatriates and the conservative bourgeoisie doubted whether a proper test of political opinion was possible in a country of such high illiteracy. In a public opinion survey conducted in the capital it was nevertheless demonstrated that urban voters were perfectly clear about the issues, about the voting symbols of the many parties, and about the name of their preferred candidate. A prediction that Nkrumah's party would win in the capital with an 80 percent landslide proved to be exactly right. Nkrumah had entered the 1954 election campaign with high optimism. His gamble in fighting the 1951 election under a constitution which he had previously denounced had paid off, and subsequently the guiding hand of Arden-

Clarke had given him parliamentary skills to add to his stature. All seemed set for him to win the election and graciously accept the grant of independence. It did not happen.

Nkrumah found that he had not yet created a unified nation out of the disparate colonial territories that had been brought together under the authority of the governor of the Gold Coast. The politics of fragmentation became a source of acute conflict in the Gold Coast for the next two years. They were Nkrumah's baptism of fire and everything that had gone so smoothly his way in 1951 seemed to turn against him in 1954. Once freedom seemed assured nationalists of every stripe fell out among themselves and squabbled fiercely over the prospective spoils. Nkrumah struggled against all the odds to win back the initiative and stand firm for a unified nation state rather than a fragmented federation. In the struggle he temporarily lost the support of some of his People's Party, of some of his British supporters, of part of the bureaucracy, and of many regional interests. One of his greatest achievements was to fight back and win the battle for unity. The election of 1954 did not itself demonstrate how hard the struggle for national integrity was going to be. Indeed Nkrumah already had his eye on the next goal, the freeing of other colonies in Africa, when suddenly he was called upon to invest all his talents and energies in the nationalist struggle at home which he had thought all but won.

The first signs of a challenge to Nkrumah developed during the 1954 election campaign. The party had had difficulty in choosing approved candidates for the single-member constituencies. Nkrumah firmly expelled eighty-one "rebel" constituency leaders who would not accept central discipline and stand down in favor of candidates approved by the national committee. Unsuccessful party men tried their hand as independent candidates and after the election became a prime source of potential recruits for a virulent new opposition party. During the election the opposition was unable to make common cause with the rebels or to match Nkrumah's appeal. The election was fought on the single issue of independence, and Nkrumah was clearly the man who had the power to deliver the promise. The hapless opposition smelt defeat before the polls even opened. The old guard could only field candidates in twenty-two constituencies and only one of them, Dr Kofi Busia, was successful. Even he, an academic with royal connections, only scraped home by eleven votes in his home town. The People's Party "rebels" did rather better and elected sixteen independents to the new assembly.

The 1954 election was emphatically won by the Convention People's Party. Gbedemah again managed a nationwide campaign backed by all the necessary logistics of transport, posters, and expenses. The party polled 55 percent of the national vote and captured seventy-two seats. It virtually swept the South, Asante, and the Volta and even in the north it won more votes, though fewer seats, than the Northern People's Party. So stunning was the victory that the opposition factions began to mobilize themselves despairingly for extra-parliamentary activity. Nkrumah was put to his first test by a storm of antagonism which blew up as suddenly and was as powerful as the coalition of favorable factors which had greeted his arrival on the scene in 1948. Had he not been a tenacious and skillful political operator he might have been swept away as quickly as he had risen.

The Constitution of the State

When Nkrumah came to power in 1951 no one in Whitehall had much idea what the nature of the postcolonial state in Africa would be. It is one of Nkrumah's greatest contributions to the history of Africa that he did have a clear vision of the kind of centralized nation that he hoped to create. Moreover he went ahead and created his unitary state in the space of six years despite challenges of every kind. The result was profound, and virtually every colony in Africa later obtained independence within the colonial frontiers that had been laid down around 1900. Minimal tinkering took place in the old German and Italian spheres but elsewhere attempts to break up colonies with new federal-type constitutions or to link colonies under new forms of control were abortive. Even the great civil wars of Nigeria, of Zaire, and of Angola ended with a restoration of the old colonial boundaries as the national frontiers. Ironically, the national norm for which Nkrumah fought so hard, the unitary state within colonial borders, became so entrenched by the 1960s that his second great objective, the creation of an African union, was effectively defeated by it.

Nkrumah had not inherited a unified territory in 1951. On the contrary the Gold Coast was divided into four rather different units, a coastal colony, a conquered kingdom, a northern protectorate, and a United Nations trust territory. One of Nkrumah's achievements was to create a sense of unity, a national identity, out of the whole, despite strong opposition both on the ground and in the Colonial Office in London. By 1957, when the country adopted the name of Ghana, there was little doubt that most citizens knew something of their new national affiliation and were proud of it. In six short years Nkrumah and his People's Party had carried Gold Coast nationalism to victory. But he had not won without a struggle. The first problem was finding a common means of communication across all the ethnic boundaries.

The achievement of a unitary state in Ghana, as in most subsequent African nations, owed a great deal to the unifying influence of the colonial language. Already in precolonial times foreign languages had been used as the means of inter-regional communication. English, in a creolized pidgin form, with a liberal dash of Portuguese vocabulary, had come to be dominant in the south. It gradually spread to the north where Arabic had been the written language of consular and diplomatic affairs and Hausa remained the commercial and military *lingua franca*. After 1900 British English increased its hold. In 1951 the nationalists had to decide whether to confirm English as their language or whether, in a burst of authenticity, to seek vernacular languages for political mobilization. Nkrumah settled for the colonial language, and the rest of Africa, with one or two partial exceptions, followed suit.

Nkrumah's decision to use English as the language of national identity, and subsequently to expand the role of English from the secondary schools into the primary schools, was not taken lightly and was always a matter of debate, at least among theoreticians. Since Ghana had about seven major languages any other choice would have been dangerously divisive. One of Nkrumah's most important campaigning slogans was "down with tribalism," and one of the major difficulties of subsequent Ghana governments was the evenhanded treatment of ethnic affairs. Since Nkrumah belonged to none of the influential ethnic groups he could not be accused of favoring his own "tribe" on any significant scale. He was neutral in disputes between the inland Asante and the Gā people of the capital. He was also free of any taint of favoritism towards the eastern Ewé, and could be nonpartisan in the affairs of coastal Fante with their long tradition of European coexistence. He could even identify with the remote north and frequently wore a northern tunic at popular rallies rather than the majestic toga favored by southern royalty.

The use of the colonial language as the language of national unification was probably justified as a political choice but it had stark social consequences. Those who had a Western schooling immediately gained the edge over those who had not. Those who lived in the town were more likely to have opportunities than those who lived in the countryside. The people of the south were far more integrated into colonial culture than the people of the north. The matter of language, therefore, had profound ideological consequences. The ideology of the People's Party was one of egalitarian socialism, but the party was run by people who spoke English and had privileged access to power, education, foreign travel, expatriate advice, and political lobbying. The sub-proletariat, the peasants, and the women were at a disadvantage compared to the clerical class, the commercial farmers, and the school-leavers, and Nkrumah opened himself to the criticism that his policy favored those already educationally advantaged. In Africa only Tanzania, which had had a triple colonial legacy of Arabs, Germans, and Britons, attempted to avoid the problem of an alienated government running the law courts, the tax administration, the local government, and the school system in a language that the majority did not understand. In West Africa the equivalent to Nyerere's Swahili would have been Hausa, and that was an unacceptable foreign language. Ghana nationalism therefore chose English.

The Crisis of Regionalism

The crisis that faced Nkrumah in 1954 was a crisis of national fragmentation. It was sprung on Ghana without apparent warning. Crises of fragmentation were to be repeated in many other African countries as the question of central loyalty versus ethnic or regional loyalty was fought out in each new nation when the cement of colonial domination was dissolved. As in so much else, Ghana faced the problem first and led the way in defending the colonial unit of administration as the proper unit of national identity. Without Nkrumah's tenacity a very different model of decolonization might have emerged. At the same time the power of the forces of fragmentation was such that central governments in Africa had to adopt strong-arm measures to overcome the centrifugal tendencies of liberation. In a few countries, such as

Sudan, the regional forces were too strong for the center to hold. In Ghana Nkrumah was able to build a convincing central power though at the cost of a considerable loss of goodwill both nationally and internationally. Expectations of a liberal democratic system of parliamentary government were eroded not so much by the dictatorial tendencies of one man or one party, but by the sudden explosion of sectional interests which showed themselves willing to jeopardize the attainment of independence if it did not further sectarian ethnic, religious, or regional interests.

Nkrumah may have been among the first to recognize, after decisively winning the election of 1954, that there were thunderclouds beyond the apparently serene horizon. On 11 August 1954 he warned the House that "if we tolerate the formation of political parties on regional, sectional or religious bases, we shall not only be heading for political chaos but, worse still, we shall be sowing the seeds of the destruction of our national existence. Coming events cast their shadows before them, and the government shall consider what steps should be taken to eradicate this emerging evil in our national life." But although Nkrumah recognized that there might be regional disaffection against his unitary nationalism he did not recognize that the bomb's fuse had already been ignited or that the crisis would begin over the price of cocoa.

The problem of all colonial economies is a problem of dependence on metropolitan markets for the sale of their raw materials. Those fortunate enough to produce several colonial products could be cushioned against some fluctuations in prices, but those that were dependent on a single crop or mineral were particularly vulnerable to the dictates of the world market. Ghana had more than one export, but the role of cocoa was nonetheless dominant in the external economy. Changes in world prices had a powerful impact, as had been seen during the cocoa "hold-ups" organized by striking farmers during the great depression. Colonial governments could manage commodity fluctuations by minimizing the publicity given to market factors, but democratic governments, which prided themselves on their openness, had much greater difficulty. This difficulty was most acute when prices fell, but Nkrumah discovered that his cocoa also caused severe turbulence when its price rose.

In 1954 the world price of cocoa reached the astronomic figure of £450 per ton. To have passed any significant part of this windfall on to the farmer, it was argued, would have led to inflation and to regional distortions of wealth. Nkrumah decided that the farmers' price should remain stable and that the surplus should be taken into government coffers to finance economic, social, industrial, political, and administrative developments in the country as a whole. He therefore announced that the farmers' price would remain at a steady £150 a ton, leaving the £300 bonus in the hands of government. The farmers were incensed, particularly after the high expectations that the election had engendered. When the government argued, oddly, that to increase the farmer's price would reduce his incentive to work, the farmers suggested wittily that the marketing board should reduce the salary of its press officer to make him work better. A black socialist government appeared to behave in accord with the classic colonial theory, propounded in South Africa, that the less people were paid the harder they would work. The cocoa farmers, not unnaturally, became militant.

The area in which militancy first broke out was Asante. Although Asante had returned eighteen Nkrumah members of parliament out of twenty-one, there was nevertheless a strong potential for the mobilization of opposition. The Asante capital, Kumasi, was the center of private enterprise and African business in Ghana. In Accra over half the population were wage earners who benefited from an expansion in the role of government. In Kumasi commerce was the principal source of livelihood and any restraint on the earning capacity of the Asante cocoa farmer was likely to limit the growth of the private commercial sector. Opposition, therefore, was not based on personality or ethnicity but on well-founded ideology and interest. The merchant city was ready to spearhead the conservative revolt of the Asante cocoa farmer against the bureaucratic bourgeoisie that benefited from a planned socialist program.

The sudden rise of Asante opposition to Nkrumah was more than a campaign for laissez-faire against central planning. It was also a move towards the devolution of power from the center to the provinces. Asante, with only one-fifth of the population of the country, possessed half of the cocoa and, incidentally, also the richest of the gold mines. By arguing for the devolution of power from the center the Asante hoped that they could hold on to a larger share of the provincial domestic product. This economically self-seeking regionalism was at the base of the storm that Nkrumah had seen brewing. But the astonishing thing about the outbreak of Asante regional politics was the extraordinarily broad coalition of sympathy and support that the leaders were able to mobilize in their favor. The first support came from other regional interests.

Regional Politics

Before 1951 the Gold Coast's four rather different territories were loosely integrated under a single colonial governor who administered the whole in four different ways. Nkrumah's ambition was to weld the four into a single nation, governed by a single parliament, elected in a single constitutional system. His success began in the coastal colony proper where his party won the municipal elections of 1950 and went on to sweep the board in the indirect "parliamentary" elections of 1951. Asante, however, was a different proposition. The heartland of the old forest kingdom had seen its royal administration gradually restored by a system of indirect rule in the 1920s, and in the 1930s the Asante king had once more acquired status and influence. The emergence of a political system based on the dispossessed, the youth, the immigrants, the landless, the town-dwellers, and the mission scholars was inimical to the old aristocracy that had so recently recovered its prestige. The Asantehene's royal court, and the provincial courts of the Asante states, were perfectly ready to lend all their weight to a movement that would oppose the young men in a hurry led by Nkrumah and his southern carpetbaggers.

Asante leaders were not alone in being ready to join a new opposition movement when they failed to win in the 1954 election. The third region in the prospective nation was the Northern Territories in the West African savanna. In the north the chiefs had quite as much influence over their subjects as the reviving aristocracy of Asante. Moreover the people were suspicious of southerners, of Western-educated administrators and politicians, of the influence of the cities. The north therefore organized its own political movement, confusingly called a people's party, like Nkrumah's party, but in practice a party of traditionalists who followed the often Muslim lead of the aristocracy. The Northern People's Party elected a significant number of members of parliament in 1954 and thus formed the official opposition. Nkrumah tried to challenge the legitimacy of an opposition that was regionally rather than nationally based, but the Speaker overruled his objections in Parliament. The north therefore provided members of parliament who were in place ready for the great challenge to Nkrumah's drive for a unitary national independence in which the economically more developed and urbanized south would lead the four regions.

The fourth region which Nkrumah had to bring into his strategic thinking was the Volta region. Constitutionally this region included the British sector of the former German colony of Togoland. Although governed by the governor of the Gold Coast, Togoland belonged juridically to the United Nations which had to decide what its political fate might be. It appeared in the perspective of the 1950s to be too small and poor to become an independent nation in its own right. An alternative option was to leap into the unknown and restore the integrity of the old German colony from which it had been carved. Such a move would have erased a controversial colonial boundary which cut through the ethnic entity of the Ewé people. It would, however, have brought British subjects under the sharply contrasted style of French colonialism which was perceived by some to be more arbitrary and more violent than the British style. A more popular case could be made for joining British Togoland to the future state of Ghana in a loose federal arrangement which gave the peoples of the Volta some political autonomy. The Volta region had elected five opposition members of parliament in 1954 for whom this option may have appeared attractive. The region had also elected eight Nkrumah supporters, one of them his most prominent deputy, Gbedemah. Their commitment to full integration into the unitary state of Ghana was the majority view. In 1956 the United Nations organized a plebiscite which endorsed integration. This left the Volta with a minority "regional" opposition which affiliated with the "tribal" opposition in Asante and the "aristocratic" opposition of the northern chiefs.

National Liberation Movement

The allied organizers of ethnic fragmentation and of economic devolution attracted powerful supporters. The old intelligentsia had been utterly routed by the more forthright school of nationalist politicians. They had not been able to offer any alternative policies to those of Nkrumah's self-government platform, but they had seriously hoped that they might be called upon as responsible elder statesmen whom the British would invite to carry policy through in a dignified rather than a populist fashion.

After losing the election they set about discrediting Nkrumah by every means at their disposal. They allied themselves to the Asante separatists, although the old intelligentsia were — with a few exceptions — actually members of the great families of the south. They argued that the unitary constitution that Nkrumah proposed was not appropriate to a country as diverse as the four territories of the Gold Coast and that the new Ghana should be federal territory with strong regional identities to protect local freedoms. They revived their old marriage of convenience with their erstwhile rivals the chiefs. But above all they tried to wean the new élite away from Nkrumah and seek a base among the mushrooming students of the country's educational institutions.

The Westernized élite of Ghana in the middle 1950s suffered from a mild degree of schizophrenia in its national identification. At one level it was intensely proud of the burgeoning new Ghana and expressed strong feelings of patriotism. It also recognized that the opportunities for personal advancement were immense as the country's administration was expanded and Africanized. When foreign businesses moved into Ghana to get a foothold in the new Africa and showed their evenhanded attitude by giving managerial positions to blacks in a manner never before dreamt of, the new élite was ready to seize its opportunity. But at the same time the educated class was antagonistic to Nkrumah. They were embarrassed by his brash political rhetoric. They spoke disparagingly of his mere American qualifications in contrast to what they imagined to be their own infinitely superior form of British training. They were also resentful that their "free" university education had to be paid for by doing five years' government service before they could seek the green pastures of private enterprise. They were arrogant about the concept of universal suffrage for illiterates. Their ambivalence led them to sympathize with the mobilization of an opposition movement.

The coalition of rebel "youngmen" from the CPP, of irate farmers, of Asante chiefs, and of discomfited intellectuals, rapidly found common cause against Nkrumah and called themselves the National Liberation Movement. Their leader, Dr. Kofi Busia, was—like Danquah before him—a university-trained anthropologist and intellectual. The Asante youth switched as quickly from Nkrumah's CPP to Busia's NLM as they had previously switched from Danquah to Nkrumah. The chiefs provided the money and a framework of ethnic support groups. The new political leaders proclaimed their aim to "banish lawlessness, intimidation, hooliganism, disregard for age and authority, suppression of individual conscience, and all traces of communism." Prominent citizens of Kumasi who had been close supporters of Nkrumah transferred their allegiance to the new movement and denounced the CPP for corruption and for the growth of a Nkrumah "personality cult." The movement acquired a strand of virulence as its action groups intimidated the Nkrumah militants with cudgels and soda bottle explosions. Within a year the movement had gained the strength of organization to win a parliamentary by-election. The aim was to stop the move towards independence and negotiate with Britain a new constitutional contract.

The leaders of the National Liberation Front believed that Britain would support their cause. In this they were encouraged by a more conservative stance in British colonial policy which culminated in the 1956 invasion of Egypt. Some colonial officials also led Busia's followers to think that Britain might wish to accept more pliant and conservative politicians as their clients on the road to independence. The governor, however, was firmly committed to the view that Nkrumah was Britain's man. In March 1955 he wrote home to his family:

About six months ago a political party calling itself the National Liberation Movement was started in Ashanti. It pretends to be a democratic organization but is in fact backed

and led by the chiefs with the Asantehene at their head. It
represents the resistance of the chiefs to the curtailment of
their own powers under the present democratic system and
their attempt to reassert their appeal to Ashanti tribal feeling which is strong. . . . They hate the CPP and are quite
determined that they will not have independence under a
CPP government, and seem prepared to go to almost any
lengths to cause the present constitution to break down.[2]

Despite the firm views of the governor the conflict did cause Britain to
arrest the process of emancipation and insist that another "independence" election be held before power be transferred. Many observers
expected Nkrumah to be defeated but they were surprised. The national results of the 1956 election came out almost identical to those of
1954. Nkrumah dropped ten seats in Asante, it is true, but he picked
up several new ones to retain his parliamentary majority. His percentage
of the national vote actually rose. There could be no further excuse to
delay independence. But the two-year hiatus had taken its toll on politicians and had altered the practice of politics in ways which were
pernicious and persistent.

The chief harm of the two-year struggle between the Nkrumah
unitarists and the Busia federalists was the introduction of violence into
the political arena. It is true that the "riot" of 1948 had done significant
damage to property, but thereafter the politics of nationalism had been
the politics of argument not the politics of personal conflict. The language of politicians and of journalists had been abusive and strident but
it was a violence of words not of arms. The Asante rebellion had
brought an element of strife to the scene as the old conservatives sought
desperately to regain the initiative. When they lost, the consequences
were dire since the third Nkrumah government could no longer assume

that opposition was going to be loyal and parliamentary. Indeed, the leader of the opposition, the smooth-spoken academic specialist in parliamentary niceties, withdrew his members from parliament during crucial phases of the independence negotiations. The precedent was unfortunate and Nkrumah was later to by-pass parliament himself. Worse still the resort to violence meant that on the eve of independence the government could not put all its creative imagination into national development but had to expend scarce political energies on questions of internal security.

Despite the virulence of opposition activity in the months before independence, the striking feature of Nkrumah's fifteen years in office was the lack of violence in Ghana. The calm which pervaded the country was not at the time seen as abnormal, and it was exceptions to the peaceful norm which attracted most attention. Unrest in Ghana was almost imperceptible compared to the violence found at the time in Asia and the Americas. Political deaths were almost unheard of in the Nkrumah era. Ghana did not have the robber bands of countries polarized by wealth, like Ethiopia, nor the civil strife of armed ideological factions, like Cameroun. It had no racial confrontations as later witnessed in Zaire or Mozambique. The serenity and stability of Ghana when banditry, revolution, and war were spreading in Africa, owes something to the pragmatic moderation of Nkrumah who steered a careful path between extremist factions, between the intelligentsia demanding more privilege and the proletariat demanding six shillings a day. The two countries which most resembled Ghana, Uganda, and Nigeria both exploded into paroxysms of self-destruction after independence, but Ghana, when the time came, removed its head of state in an almost bloodless coup with dancing in the streets rather than shootings and lynchings. The next generation of politicians was not as successful as Nkrumah had been at maintaining national harmony and avoiding bloodshed.

The Transfer of Power

Although the federalist rebellion somewhat soured Britain's relations with Ghana in general and with Nkrumah in particular, it could not in any way be claimed that Nkrumah had failed to win a fair election on a fair platform of national unity and independence. Sections of the British establishment and media nevertheless felt duped when their predictions of a federalist victory proved wrong and so they fueled a campaign of denigration against Nkrumah. The words rather than the deeds of the opposition were broadcast to the West, and Nkrumah was somehow portrayed as a threat to democracy rather than its champion. The effects of this must have been harmful. Nkrumah had collaborated with the British in every way, except perhaps in taming the anti-colonial enthusiasm of the press. Even here, however, he was caught in a bind and would surely have been accused of totalitarianism had he tried to censor the wilder statements of his followers. Nkrumah came to be seen in Whitehall as the black sheep who could do no right. No way could be found of denying his independence, but there was an element of grudge against his success. The British press were never as successful at blackening Nkrumah's name as they were to be in blackening the name of Africa's other uncompromising nationalist, Nasser of Egypt, but it nevertheless created a sour taste in the mouth of many observers. Nkrumah was not subservient enough, obsequious enough, to be the first heir to an African colony. He even committed the heinous crime of talking about neocolonialism and, however much the British tried to ridicule the idea that they were giving with one hand to take back with the other, the reality of the neocolonial nexus came to dawn slowly on Africa watchers everywhere.

Despite the reluctance and suspicion, Britain did proceed with the arrangements for independence after the 1956 election. It probably had no choice. The fiasco of the Suez War had ended once and for all any attempt to try to restore old-style colonialism. Even if Britain had not understood that for itself, the matter would have been made clear by the United States. America was anxious to see the European powers weaken their hold on the old colonies and allow transatlantic business to expand into Africa. But in Britain itself a new generation had taken the helm. At their head was Harold Macmillan. He knew that a wind of change was blowing through Africa and that a whole new set of partnerships between the industrial world and the developing world would have to be built. Indeed, he first gave his "wind of change" speech in Accra at a dinner hosted by Nkrumah. The content was so obvious that no one much noticed. It was only when he repeated it a few days later in Cape Town that his white hosts took exception and the phrase reverberated around the world.

Once the die was cast, and the Westminster parliament had enacted the Gold Coast independence legislation, preparations for celebration burst out across the length and breadth of Ghana. Nkrumah's new nation was to be the most exuberant of all the African countries. Pride and good humor were the hallmarks of its nationalism.

3

National Statesman

At zero hundred hours on 6 March 1957 Nkrumah proclaimed to a jubilant throng assembled on the old Accra polo ground that Ghana was free. It was an occasion of high emotion and of far-reaching significance. World representatives came from every corner to witness the occasion and President Eisenhower even sent the vice president of the United States, Richard Nixon, to present his blessing. Six hundred journalists descended on Africa, most of them for the first time in their lives. The new red, yellow, and green bunting was flown everywhere. A national anthem was performed by bands throughout the country. The prime minister's stalwart lieutenants shared his glory on the tribune. The crowds sang the nationalist hymns and danced in the streets. Governor Arden-Clarke was invited to become the new head of state with the title of governor-general representing the Queen. Constitutional niceties were thereby observed and the elders were given due honor by the young radicals. Amidst all the celebrations few had the foresight to recognize that independence day was the beginning of the struggle and not its end. Only much later did freedom fighters in

Mozambique devise the slogan *"a luta continua,"* recognizing full well that the transfer of power gave the opportunity to face the problem of national development but provided none of the solutions. Nkrumah had to learn the hard way, as the pioneer of African independence, that freedom presented bitter challenges.

The domestic program which Nkrumah set for Ghana was one of industrialization. With hindsight this may or may not have been an intelligent choice, but in 1957 it seemed to him the best path by which his people could be drawn out of rural poverty. His experience of the developed world had been gained in the old coal-fired industrial communities of Pennsylvania and Britain. The most radical model of economic growth available to date appeared to be the electrification of the Soviet Union. Nkrumah thought that industry must be his path and that electrical energy was the fuel of the future. The people of Ghana will never be happy, he said, until industrial smoke and grime make it impossible to see from one side of the Volta River to the other. He dusted off old colonial reports on how to build a giant hydroelectric project on Ghana's river and harness it to his industrial revolution.

The Volta River Project

The Volta River Project was the largest scheme associated with Nkrumah's development plans, and one of the largest investment projects hitherto contemplated in Africa. It was to be his monument, but also his Waterloo. He sank not only many of the country's now dwindling assets, and an expensive tranche of loan capital, into the scheme but also a large portion of his political credibility. The project symbolized all his ideals for a prosperous future, but it also became an obsession and later a debt for the next generation. The achievements of the Volta scheme, and its flaws, explain much about Africa in the neocolonial age. Hydroelectricity was widely recognized as the best potential energy for

Africa since coal reserves were scarce and only economically viable in the super-exploited labor conditions of southern Africa. Petroleum was also scarce in Africa before the great oil strikes in Libya and Nigeria, and Ghana never found oil in commercial quantity. Uranium, which was to become the great export of Africa in the 1970s, had not yet been harnessed as a nuclear fuel, and hydroelectric dams thus seemed the only way to industrialize.

The building of dams involved intense diplomacy at a level to which new African statesmen were as yet unaccustomed, and several of Africa's great dams were the cause of war. The Aswan high dam on the Nile triggered the Suez War in which Britain lost its bid to remain an old-style imperial power, and the Soviet Union brought its cold war with America into Africa. Two very large Zambezi dams later accentuated wars in Mozambique and Rhodesia in a struggle to protect cheap electricity for white-owned mining industries. Nkrumah entered this world of diplomacy and engineering, of conflict and high finance, with a naïve innocence. He confidently assumed that his electricity would be cheaper than any alternative and that customers would be knocking at his door. The technical difficulties of creating the largest man-made lake in the world were, however, such as to cast doubt on the cost-effectiveness of the scheme, and the necessary scale of the enterprise meant finding buyers for a million kilowatts of power with no Copperbelt or Witwatersrand nearby. Domestic and industrial consumption in Ghana and the adjacent French territories was tiny compared to lower Egypt served by Aswan electricity. Even the gold mines were too small and distant to be ideal customers. The Volta project therefore sought a future in the aluminum industry.

Nkrumah's first attempt to raise finance for an integrated industrial complex based on an aluminum smelter failed. During the early 1950s energy prices were falling in relation to other industrial costs, and aluminum prices were not rising as anticipated. Much more seriously the Gold Coast was the victim of neocolonial manipulations even before it had achieved independence. Western industry wanted to keep its Volta River option on "hold" while it explored the profit margins elsewhere. In particular the West wanted to see what opportunities new technology would create for aluminum smelting in conservative Canada rather than in unknown Africa. Nkrumah was the mouse while industry played cat. A radical black politician was not seen as the ideal partner unless profits were very high and expropriation risks severely discounted. The scheme was stalled for bad political reasons as well as some sound economic ones so long as the Gold Coast remained under tutelage. After independence the project surfaced again and Nkrumah, now unfettered, put all his weight behind it.

Nkrumah, better than anyone else of his generation, understood the realities of the neocolonial thinking of which he was the victim. But if he wanted to free Ghana from its dependence on cocoa, and on the vagaries of raw commodity and agricultural prices, by attracting investment, he had to negotiate terms with the industrial powers, and most especially with the United States. The story is told of how, soon after independence, Nkrumah's finance minister, Gbedemah, traveled through America and entered, wittingly or unwittingly, into a chain café which had a policy of refusing to serve blacks. The embarrassing press publicity of having a distinguished visiting statesman bounced from a public place was so severe that Gbedemah was invited to breakfast at the White House. The whole caper may have been deliberately engineered by the minister's Afro-American private secretary, but it led Eisenhower to think personally about Africa. Having so recently lost its dominant influence in China, America was anxious not to drive Africa into the arms of the Soviet Union. Eisenhower requested that American industry reexamine the feasibility of the Volta project. The

Kaiser corporation took up the invitation, recommended a better dam site, and proposed that an aluminum smelter be sited on the coast beside a new deep-water port. The strings, however, were very firmly attached: the corporation would not be interested in the project if it were to be an integrated industrial complex under the actual or potential control of indigenous politicians.

The American proposal for a Volta project was to split the scheme in two and put each half in a different country to preclude national control or expropriation. Nkrumah's plan had been to develop an integrated aluminum industry based not only on Volta power but also on raw Ghana bauxite. This the Americans would not contemplate. They would only build a smelter if it was at the port where foreign semi-processed ore from Jamaica could be imported and the finished product exported. The only Ghana input would be electricity. The Ghana bauxite mines would be "frozen" for ten years while the financiers tested the temper of the politicians. The aluminum would be taken out in ingots rather than turned into finished goods. The Ghana share of the value added would be minimal and the only attraction was the prospect of an energy base for the long-term future. These terms were tough, but worse was to come as the Americans realized the depth of Nkrumah's commitment to the project, for which he would pay almost any price. The price they finally extorted was that Nkrumah would contribute £35 million of Ghana's own peasant-based resources and pay a steep rate of interest on a loan of £80 million supplied by America, Britain, the World Bank, and an aluminum consortium established to buy the power. Nkrumah was an early victim of the capitalist realization that lending to the Third World could be extremely profitable and that debtor nations in Africa had little political power with which to protect themselves.

Negotiating a loan to build the dam was not Nkrumah's only

problem in dealing with America. Before being offered a contract he was severely pressed to keep the price of the resulting electricity down to an uneconomic level. The World Bank advised him that at one-third of a penny per unit the return on capital would be only 3 percent, hardly an interesting profit even in the 1950s. Other users would be expected to pay three half-pence a unit, four times as much. The aluminum consortium, however, refused to offer even the lower price and claimed adamantly that there was over-capacity in the world aluminum industry, and that they could not and would not pay more than a quarter of a penny. They also hinted to Nkrumah that the World Bank had been unduly pessimistic in its calculations and they quite falsely dangled the prospect of a spiraling economic spin-off. Nkrumah succumbed.

The development potential of the Volta River Project need not have been an illusion. There was, however, never adequate evaluation of the public relations talk of irrigation, fishing, lake transport, electrically based manufacturing, high-tension lines to the mines or sale of energy to neighboring countries. The Volta project was uncritically expected to be the source of all future wealth. It also drew the attention of scarce economists, planners, administrators, expatriates, politicians, and even journalists away from broader if more mundane opportunities that Ghana might have considered. It suited the flamboyant style of Nkrumah whose admirers called him "showboy" and expected his achievements to be as spectacular in economics as they had been in politics. Preoccupation with the Volta led to a neglect of the cocoa industry and a higher taxation of cocoa farmers to pay the cost. This accentuated the regional differences, with the Volta project concentrated in the southeast and the cocoa revenues increasingly being drawn from the devolutionist Asante region. The government forged ahead regardless and instead of rescuing Ghana from its economic underdevelopment hastened national bankruptcy and the exhaustion of the reserves.

One of the explanations for Nkrumah's commitment to the Volta project concerns his political style of close personal attachment to his associates. As a black apprentice politician Nkrumah had been inspired by George Padmore. As a leader of government business he had been guided by Sir Charles Arden-Clarke. Now as a national statesman responsible for economic development Nkrumah fell under the magnetic charm of the American tycoon, Edgar Kaiser. One of the honest brokers in the partnership was Dame Barbara Ward, the foremost development economist of her day, a friend of the rising Kennedy family, and incidentally the wife of the Volta project's director. Kaiser understood Nkrumah's psychology well, his need to be liked, his need to be associated with famous and powerful world figures, and so conducted his corporate raid of Ghana with such finesse that the nationalist black leader was charmed. The Volta project's public relations spokesman, James Moxon, assessed the cost:

> Edgar Kaiser saw in the fantastically cheap electric power
> that he alone, with his dual expertise as a dam builder and
> as an aluminum producer, could extract from Ghana, the
> opportunity to bring untold riches to his family business.
> And at the same time Kwame Nkrumah knew, after a num-
> ber of grim disappointments, that it was only the unique
> power of American capital backing the skills and enthusi-
> asm of the Kaiser consortium that would give him the
> entrée to a new industrial economy that was his cherished
> goal for Ghana. And even though he disliked intensely the
> ideology of US capitalism and later on believed that it had
> cheated him of the wider industrial economy that he had

set his heart on, in favor of a single American-owned enclave which was essentially self-prospering, he too pulled out every stop to fulfil his dreams. Thus the Nkrumah-Kaiser "rapport" was born and indeed flourished and if, in truth, it was more in the nature of cupboard love than a fusion of hearts it was nevertheless a very real force and, most certainly, changed the course of Ghana history.[3]

The Volta dam was completed on 22 January 1966. Nkrumah ceremonially opened it in a blaze of world publicity. He did not know that his time was up and that his presidency had less than one month to run.

Economic Planning

While the Volta dam was being built, during Nkrumah's last five years in office, a fierce debate about economic strategy exercised academic economists. One school, partly echoing the strident claims of Nkrumah's opponents in exile, argued that after 1961 economic policy was essentially concerned with the rewarding of supporters and with the appeasing of groups who might challenge the presidential authority. The argument went so far as to propound a cynical thesis that West African policymakers in general were concerned first and foremost to enrich the ruler, the ministers, the party leaders and the civil servants.

A sharply contrasted school claimed, however, that Nkrumah conspicuously failed either to reward his key followers or to buy off his most dangerous opponents. His policy was much more in line with the received wisdom of mainstream development economists who argued that austerity in the short term was necessary to achieve prosperity in the long term. In 1961 increases in taxation, and the introduction of compulsory national savings, were unpopular long-term strategies which caused strikes and protests rather than giving instant rewards to the faithful. Two years later international economic advisers of very diverse persuasions endorsed the broad industrializing direction of Nkrumah's seven-year development plan.

The great development urgency which Nkrumah adopted in the 1960s was a break with the continuities of economic policy and pragmatic decision-making which he had inherited from the Colonial Office. He had now been in power for ten years and faced what became the classic dilemma of how to maintain the momentum of the anticolonial crusade in the field of development. The country expected miracles — indeed had been promised miracles and Nkrumah had to create the wealth to satisfy the expectations he had called forth. In trying to force the pace a few of the more conservative party leaders were replaced by radical men, and the stalwart minister of finance, Gbedemah, was demoted in the government and soon after fled the country to become an exiled opponent of his erstwhile associate.

At each level of planning a choice had to be made between private enterprise and public initiative. Among the party faithful the "modernizers" pushed themselves to the fore, anxious to improve their economic and class status. Nkrumah, however, decided against fostering an indigenous entrepreneurial class. He argued that Ghana's chances of generating enough private capital to industrialize rapidly were too slender. Only small-scale production and distribution were to be left in the hands of traditional family firms, of market women, or of immigrant business people from Lebanon and Nigeria. Industry and the commanding heights of the economy would need to be state-sponsored, financed out of taxation and if necessary bolstered by government-controlled foreign investment. In spite of the prevalent African ambivalence towards the "aid" nexus, Nkrumah anticipated that overseas capital and management would be needed to finance his import-substitution industries, his mechanized farm schemes, his state-run wholesale businesses.

Nkrumah's search to balance the conflicting objectives of socialism, economic independence and industrial modernization grew from
the credo enunciated in his 1957 autobiography:

> The ideology of my Party may be formulated as follows: no
> race, no people, no nation can exist freely and be respected
> at home and abroad without political freedom.
>
> Once this freedom is gained, a greater task comes into
> view. All dependent territories are backward in education,
> in science, in agriculture, and in industry. The economic in-
> dependence that should follow and maintain political inde-
> pendence demands every effort from the people, a total
> mobilization of brain and manpower resources. What other
> countries have taken three hundred years or more to
> achieve, a once dependent territory must try to accomplish
> in a generation if it is to survive. Unless it is, as it were,
> "jet-propelled," it will lag behind and thus risk everything
> for which it has fought.
>
> Capitalism is too complicated a system for a newly inde-
> pendent nation. Hence the need for a socialistic society.[4]

The Gold Mines

Nkrumah faced international difficulties not only in creating a new
industrial sector for Ghana, but also in establishing control over the old
industry of gold mining. The gold mines were important, and indeed
Ghana was named after a medieval gold-trading empire in the southern
Sahara. By the fifteenth century gold from the forest mines of the Gold
Coast was reaching the Muslim world by donkey and camel and the
Christian world by Portuguese ocean caravel. Hand digging and stream
washing continued until the late nineteenth century when dynamite

and pumps facilitated deep level mining. Foreign capital, technology, and management created jobs for tens of thousands of laborers and thousands of craftsmen. Gold was second only to cocoa as a source of foreign exchange. But for mining capital to win an appreciable profit it had to keep wages low, and in the 1920s the otherwise enlightened Governor Guggisberg found it expedient to authorize the recruitment of forced labor rather than forego the benefits of mineral royalties with which to finance his development program. During the Great Depression and the World War the industry continued to be modeled on South African patterns of exploitation, but in 1944 a trade union was formed, under artisan leadership, and by 1947 the mine workers were ready to strike back at the mine owners. The union won its first battle a month before Nkrumah arrived in Africa. Despite powerful opposition from the Chamber of Mines, 30,000 miners won concessions that included not only a pay rise but also leave entitlements, sick pay, overtime, a forty-five hour week, and end-of-service gratuities. Trade unionism had proved itself against the most powerful employers' ring in the colony.

The Chamber of Mines began to fight back despite the unpropitious climate of political change. It sought to protect its tax advantages, to reduce its dependence on cheap labor by mechanization, to denounce the "poisonous doctrines" of the young nationalists, to intimidate union activists. But it also began to realize that a more thoughtful and subtle approach to the new politics was required. The initiative was taken by General Spears, chairman of the richest mine and reputed to be a hardliner even by colonial standards. He unexpectedly turned to paternalism, to welfare programs, and to feeding schemes in an attempt to create worker loyalty to his mine. He also turned to the politics of propaganda and went so far as to counter the nationalist movement by launching his own newspaper, the *Ashanti Times*. As he explained to the editor:

It is well known that the selection of news is one of the
most powerful weapons of propaganda, and by selecting
and emphasizing the right sort of news, and by editorials,
which while not being direct propaganda would influence
opinion in the right direction, much can be done to fulfill
the essential purpose of this newspaper which is to build up
a body of opinion interested in and loyal to the mine. . . .
In so far as the newspaper is not able to do anything to
build up the morale of the workers or to strengthen the
co-operation between the management and the workers or
to enlighten public opinion about the problems facing management, it is not justified in its existence. World news and
features should be the sugar on the pill.[5]

This mine owner who understood about media manipulation decided to
go further and to work within the framework of the new politics by
establishing a personal rapport with Kwame Nkrumah, the leader whose
career was partly based on his profile in the press. Spears embarked on a
process of subtle friendship and influence that undermined Nkrumah's
independent judgment of the mining industry in general and of the
Ashanti Goldfield Corporation in particular. This "corruption" did not,
as far as is known, take the form of payments, backhanders, bribes, world
travel, or numbered bank accounts, but was innocently directed at
Nkrumah's personality. General Spears made it his widely publicized custom to give Nkrumah sophisticated mechanical toys as Christmas pres-
ents. They were more a joke than a bribe to the outside observer, but they
served their political function exceedingly well. By the time the gold
miners were ready to embark on their second major strike the chairman
of the leading mine was on friendly terms with the black prime minister
who represented all the ideals that he most loathed.

The role of Spears in the Nkrumah story is an important one in that it pointed the way for a very much larger and more effective British entrepreneur in Africa. "Tiny" Rowlands, like Spears before him, recognized the power of the press and so bought his way into the newspapers of new nations in Africa. He went further and bought his way into the liberal press of Britain as well, thus preparing a sugar coating for his ideas. He followed Spears in getting to know his enemies, the black political leaders, and pragmatically capturing their friendship. His Lonrho corporation took over the Ashanti Goldfields, spread its methods widely in Africa and was dubbed "the unacceptable face of capitalism" by Edward Heath. But neither moral condemnation nor association with the pariah politicians of South Africa limited the effectiveness of private enterprise penetration in Africa. Nkrumah may have been the first African leader to be seduced by a new generation of British neocolonial tycoons. He was certainly not the last.

State Power and Union Power

Nkrumah's great conflict with the workers came in 1955, even before he had won independence. The gold miners called a second great strike, but this time the nationalists were in government and their attitude to the dispute was more nuanced than in 1947. On one side the nationalists needed foreign exchange and tax revenues from the mine companies, but on the other side they were the radical party elected to defend the people against imperialism personified by its mining agents. Spears leant on his friend Nkrumah who in turn leant on the miners' president, but still the hundred-day strike dragged on. The companies took dramatic action, permanently flooded two mines, and plausibly threatened that if government did not help them keep labor costs down they would abandon Ghana on the eve of independence and deprive it of all gold revenue. It was Nkrumah's first harsh experience of life at the top.

He could influence neither the unions nor the companies. Industrial relations took their course, and a compromise one shilling rise was agreed, but the prime minister had read the warning. There were forces in Ghana still beyond the reach of Nkrumah's politics. Once independence was assured, much of his political effort therefore had to be devoted first of all to controlling the trade union movement and secondly to managing the mining industry.

In the aftermath of the great mine strike Nkrumah set about reducing the autonomous power of trade union leadership. The ruling party, for all its radical socialist rhetoric, was committed to attracting overseas capital and to a policy of industrialization. To do this Nkrumah needed to convince potential investors that he was willing to control wage demands, and demonstrate his ability to do so in the one existing industrial sector, mining. A policy of institutional labor control suited a ruling party which feared the rivalry of an independent trade union movement. The government limited the bargaining power of the mine workers by bringing the union under the control of a now party-dominated Trade Union Congress and by co-opting the powerful mine union president into the privileged élite of party stalwarts. A trade union act of 1958 effectively outlawed strikes. Trade union membership became restive as it saw its leaders collaborating with management and government. By 1961 workers were calling for strike action against a government which had not only repressed their freedom, but had failed to call forth the promised economic dawn. The lead was taken on this occasion not by the miners but by the railway workers.

The railway workers of the Gold Coast had been successfully unionized since the 1920s and had learned how to use strikes to advance their cause and send political signals to whatever government was in power. At the end of the war it was they who had organized an autonomous Trade Union Congress. In 1950 the railway workers supported

Nkrumah and his People's Party. His "positive action" call for self-government, though receiving limited support from other sections of organized labor, was supported by an effective rail strike. On that occasion two weeks of paralysis convinced the colonial government that it would have to make political concessions and led the party to believe that the "workers" were its allies. Railwaymen had played a significant part in the making of Kwame Nkrumah and by 1961 were ready to call in the debt. Inflation was again high and wage-earners were feeling the pinch of consumer shortages much as they had done in the turbulent year 1948. The railway strike of September 1961 was not only about wage grievances, however, but was also a political strike. The unions were protesting about economic policy and increased taxation. The strike lasted seventeen days and unleashed the most powerful challenge the independent government had yet faced. It speeded Nkrumah's transition from hero to villain in the eyes of the proletariat.

Nkrumah, like a new parent with no models to follow except those by which he had himself been raised, responded to the trade union challenge in much the same way as any undemocratic colonial administration might have done. He declared a state of emergency in old-fashioned British style. The country had come full circle, but this time it was Nkrumah who was doing the prison detaining rather than being himself detained as had happened in the strike of 1950. Strike leaders and opposition politicians were arrested in a show of coercive force that no governor could have bettered. Party zealots penetrated the union movement with corrosive cynicism. Dock workers were particularly victimized since they lived in municipal cities where their radical anti-government ideas could easily infect the urban population. The mine workers found themselves in a peculiarly invidious position since many were by now the employees of a state corporation which had nationalized some of the gold mines.

Nationalization

The nationalization of a section of the gold-mining industry was one of the turning points of Nkrumah's career. It once again demonstrated the narrow room for maneuver that was permitted to national leaders in small countries which, despite their flag independence and their fancy constitutions, were economically dependent on foreign nations or corporations. After the 1955 strike the mine companies recognized that under black ministers they could not keep wages down effectively and so they began abandoning marginal mines to protect profits and refrained from investing risk money in modernization. In 1960, rather than face the closure of more of his mines, Nkrumah offered to nationalize the least profitable sections of the industry. The scenario was similar to Britain in the 1940s where capital offered little resistance to the nationalization of unprofitable industries which might provide a subsidized service to profitable industries in private hands. But Nkrumah was forced to pay dearly for the feeble end of the industry which he wanted to protect even though gold prices were still pegged at thirty-five dollars an ounce. The bargain obtained was a poor one which the country could ill afford when other priorities cried out for investment, when reserves were running low, and when the price of cocoa was dropping. Gold, however, mesmerized politicians as much in Ghana as it did in Britain. Mine nationalization as a step to industrialization and as a means of preserving foreign exchange proved even less rational when it emerged that General Spears's mine had been exempted from state control.

The Ashanti Goldfields were not only the richest of the Ghana mines, but among the richest gold mines in the world. The gold yield per ton of rock was twenty times that of the admittedly very much larger mines of South Africa. This was the one mine from which real national benefit might have been drawn, but if Nkrumah had nationalized the

Ashanti Goldfields he would have faced a barrage of world criticism and a concerted financial assault. When Nasser nationalized the Suez Canal, with full compensation, he was so effectively branded a dangerous extremist that even liberals and socialists shied away from him for years afterwards. Had Nkrumah nationalized a mine that international capital was not willing to release he would have jeopardized his whole industrial dream. Instead he was left holding the dud mines which Ghana could not afford either to keep open or to close down. It was not surprising that Nkrumah's philosophy study group agonized over an understanding of neocolonialism.

Nationalization in a new country inevitably presented difficulties, but because Nkrumah came first he was personally blamed for problems which ought more properly to have been seen as structural or generic. His personal inadequacies in the huge role for which he had been cast were genuine enough, but his scope for maneuver was far narrower than was then imagined. One problem was the "localization" of management when Africans with experience of accountability were scarce in the plethora of new state-controlled bureaucracies. The other was the ongoing confrontation with the unions. In Africa, as in the Soviet Union, trade unions were now expected to support the national effort rather than defend sectional interests, and "African socialism" came to mean state capitalism.

> Nkrumah now regarded the trade unions as mobilizers of
> the country's human resources, and declared in 1962 that
> their "former role of struggling against capitalists is obso-
> lete." They were now to "inculcate in our working people
> the love for labour and increased productivity." This doc-
> trine was faithfully echoed in the speeches of the Mine
> Workers' Union leaders. In April 1963 Foevie [the presi-

dent of the union] announced that the union's new slogans should be "increased productivity, higher efficiency, more discipline"; "the union now has a new task. They have to teach the workers that they belong to the industry — it is the duty of the union to assist management in improving skills and to make every worker share the responsibility of getting work done, rather than always being critical of management."[6]

Union members did not take kindly to productivity deals which were designed to improve the national economy and demonstrate loyalty to the national leadership rather than improve their pay packets, their rations, their housing, their safety levels. Trouble erupted in 1964 and the now sinking government declared a one-party state to minimize organized mass protest. In the mines the hero of the 1955 strike was made managing director and president of the Chamber of Mines. He systematically set about destroying his old union and replacing it with party committees, thus giving substance to complaints that Ghana was becoming a one-party dictatorship. Apart from General Spears's private mine the mines continued to run as subsidized loss-makers, winning some foreign exchange and avoiding redundancies but not offering a living wage. Confrontation between the miners and the party intensified until the February 1966 *coup d'état*.

Food and Agriculture
The problems of industry affected only a small part of the population of Ghana. A much greater problem in the 1960s was the problem of food farming. Colonial society had not created any significant urban population supplied by agricultural industries, and subsistence farming was the dominant source of food. When urbanization grew in pace

Nkrumah had to seek an agricultural policy. One solution was to spe-
cialize in export commodities — cocoa, timber, minerals — and buy cheap
food from the wheat basket of North America. This conventional strategy was adopted on a small scale until foreign exchange ran low. An
alternative policy, abortively tried at the time by Khrushchev in southern Russia, was the opening of virgin farm land to collectivized enterprise. Nkrumah attempted this too but found, as did Nyerere in East
Africa, that bureaucrats made dangerously incompetent agricultural
planners. The third strategy, tried by Mao in the Chinese cultural revolution, was to compel city youth to go and work on the land. This led
to great resistance. Nkrumah had won strong support from young men
who had left the country to find a better life in the town. To now
compel them to go back to work on the farms, or in the government
worker brigades, was to court disastrous unpopularity. Attempts to reverse the urban drift led to authoritarian measures and rebellious protests in Ghana as elsewhere in Africa. Economic rationality showed that
even low levels of under-employment in town were more rewarding
than most kinds of rural work.

One way of improving farm incomes was to improve rural marketing systems. No country, however, had satisfactory experience in
creating state-run agencies for linking provincial supply with urban
demand. Ghana, like the rest of Africa, was short on managerial com-
petence for such enterprises. Private enterprise, on the other hand, was
not favored by government, and was also short of talent. Men who
went into salaried government employment were not encouraged, as
they were in Kenya, to undertake side ventures in private enterprise.
The buying and carrying of food was largely left to women and to
Lebanese who resented government restriction or competition. The
farmers' brigades were politically unpopular and economically irrele-
vant. They also drained off significant government funds in inappropri-

ate technological investment which showed low return and had high running costs for spares and fuel. Nkrumah had no more success than any other Third World, or indeed Second World, country in revolutionizing the broad rural base of his nation. By sending people back to the land he sowed the seeds of resistance in the very core of his admiring "verandah boy" constituency.

Hero Worship

One of the criticisms leveled at Nkrumah concerned his encouragement of a "personality cult." The charge was both fair and unfair. Nkrumah did capture the limelight, and had he not done so would not have achieved his great triumphs in speeding Ghana and Africa to independence. But it was not only Nkrumah who was presented in personal terms. Most Ghanaian — and African — politics were presented in terms of personality. Policy was much more difficult to get across to the electorate than the success — or failure — of an individual. Nkrumah had managed to present policy issues early in his career by sticking to one simple message: Freedom. When the issues became more difficult he had little option but to exhort his followers to trust him in the complex negotiations of statesmen. The people of Ghana discussed their politics in terms of the personalities of ministers, rather than in terms of policy objectives. Not only was policy presented in terms of the personal aims of individual politicians, but ideology was personalized too. Nkrumah, like a Lenin or a Mao, wanted to be seen as the great ideological thinker of Africa, the proponent of the African personality in politics.

Nkrumah's attempts to create a corpus of ideological thinking, once the simple issue of independence had been resolved, did not have great success. At Government House he chaired an academic study group devoted to the wider philosophical issues of Africa, but unlike the simple winning message of 1957, the thoughts of "Chairman

Kwame" were obscurely arcane. Several collaborative authors ghosted books for him, notably *Consciencism,* but they were mocked by intellectuals and ignored by the public. He was forced to return to the simpler style: the message is the man. Nkrumah took on the title Osagyefo, and was accused of blasphemy by fundamentalist mission converts who thought he presented himself as a messiah. Increasingly he appeared to the middle class as ridiculously self-important. And yet once again he had little choice but to personalize politics, and his successors across the continent did the same. Kenyatta became Mzee, the elder, Nyerere became Mwalimu, the teacher, and Mobutu, the soldier-president, carried idolatry yet further. Even in Mozambique a leader who was genuinely anxious to emphasize ideology rather than personality soon found that every expectation was placed in him personally: "All will be well when Machel comes down from the north." Hero-worship was as old as politics itself and Nkrumah was unfairly blamed for setting the trend in Africa.

Nkrumah's private life was more modest than his flamboyant political image. In his early years as leader his home had been spartan. A young hanger-on acted as his houseboy and cooked meals which he ate at unconventional hours or while attending to the constant throng of supplicants who tried to see him in his little house. Not until after independence did he marry, and then he chose as his bride a young Egyptian Christian who spoke French rather than English. The marriage was a diplomatic match rather than a love match, but both parents enjoyed their children who grew up to be both Egyptian and Ghanaian but who also inherited their father's attachment to Britain and things British. Much earlier Nkrumah had had a son outside of marriage and he became a medical doctor and was at his father's side when he died.

Nkrumah's friends broadened his cultural horizons beyond the reading of philosophy and the entertaining of his study circle. Erica

Powell shared her love of classical music with him. Other friends introduced him to tennis and persuaded him to take greater care of his health and his diet. In later years he became rather obsessed with health and would put off his weekly meeting with the Queen's representative if there was so much as a suggestion that the noble earl was suffering from a head cold. Travel played an important part in Nkrumah's life and he undertook strenuous and at times extravagant journeys to most parts of the world while in office. His entourage did not always enjoy the experience as much as he did while they gossiped and plotted their progress through Russia or India or America. Nkrumah became keenly interested in gardening and when he went into exile in Guinea in 1966 he cultivated the roses at the villa which was granted to him as honorary co-president of his country of refuge. In exile he continued to welcome visitors and his impulsive hospitality was apparently as spontaneous as ever. Friends also nurtured a more serious, more spiritual, side to the man. Before important occasions he liked to meditate in silence, alone or with a companion whom he would summon by telephone at unexpected hours of the morning. This private man, however, was eclipsed by the media hero who won elections.

In the 1960s the hero-worship of Nkrumah was followed by a biting backlash. The Nkrumah who could do no wrong, the Nkrumah who shall never die, gradually became Nkrumah the anti-hero. The cocoa farmers turned against him when too much of their profit margin was taxed for national policies in which they saw little personal benefit. The trade unions turned against him when he tried to replace wage incentives with patriotic duty as a spur to hard work and productivity. The market women turned against him when the supply of manufactured goods dried up in the warehouses because foreign exchange was being expended on long-term projects rather than on consumer satisfaction. Worse still, the retailers found great resistance to the manufactured products of import-substitution industries which Nkrumah had fostered. Wage-earners wanted Danish lager and Dutch wax prints rather than Star beer and "made-in-here" mammy cloth. Salary-earners wanted refrigerators and above all private motor cars.

One of the most harmful legacies of colonialism in Africa was the material lifestyle of its white rulers. In countries with national incomes of a few hundred pounds per head expatriates expected to live in more than bourgeois comfort. When they orchestrated a transfer of power to a national bourgeoisie molded in their own image they transferred the expectation of a similar lifestyle. This was partly unconscious and partly a deliberate creation of cultural values which would have beneficial consequences in terms of diplomatic solidarity and commercial intercourse. The consequence was a catastrophic polarization of wealth in Africa. African bureaucrats expected to drive private cars when those of the much richer Soviet Union went by bus and those of China had to save for years to afford a bicycle. Scaling down the material expectation of the élite was a thing that few African politicians were hardy enough to attempt. Nkrumah did so with peculiar ineptitude. He allowed his closest associates to wax fat while everyone else suffered in a climate of austerity. He thus created jealousy as well as perceived deprivation. The middle class, which had prospered most under Nkrumah's program of nation building, became his most bitter critic.

Preventive Detention

The rising tide of opposition to Nkrumah increasingly caused him to see dissidents, enemies, and even subversive plotters behind every criticism or protest. As early as 1958 a curious incident surfaced. A member of the parliamentary opposition was accused of trying to buy military accouterments in London with a view to infiltrating the army. This was the first sign of potential violence in an otherwise peaceful and good-humored country. The plot may well have been an illusion, but Nkrumah believed that someone had intended to assassinate him as he left on a "pilgrimage" to India. Hitherto no statesman had ever been assassinated in Africa and the prospect caused unaccustomed tremors. A protracted legal enquiry was undertaken, but without conclusive results. Nkrumah became a more fearful man. He also lost faith in the democratic system of British justice and was tempted to return to the certainties of the colonial system. In 1958 he got parliament to pass a "preventive detention" act.

One of the enduring legacies of the British in Africa, and one which was to prove a thorn in the side of many nationalists, was the legal system. British justice was partly designed to discourage social change and so was potentially unhelpful to radical politicians of both left as in Ghana, and right as in South Africa. Under colonialism the rule of law had often been neglected as the protection of liberties was not well entrenched. Although governors, and even district commissioners, were not always respectors of *habeas corpus,* the colonial legal structures nevertheless bequeathed an enduring system of magistrates to the nationalists. Nkrumah felt hampered by laws protecting the interests of the educated and the privileged, and hankered after the certainties which colonial governors could allow themselves when dealing with political dissent. Like many nationalist politicians he became restive when impartial decisions were handed down by judges and so began to short-circuit the rule of law in the fear that opposition in Africa was likely to be seditious rather than loyal. The confrontation with the law led to the dismissal of judges. This dangerous path was later followed by others, but Nkrumah himself drew the line at extra-judicial violence. When his successors were frustrated by the law they so threatened their opponents that some lawyers fled the country in fear of their lives. Under Nkrumah no "hit squad" intimidated the judiciary or the opposition though the threat of prison caused a serious hardening of hostility to the president's men.

No single measure did more to bring down Nkrumah's reputation than his adoption of internment without trial for the preservation of security. No other measure led to such vilification at home and abroad, not his financial misjudgments, nor his extravagant prestige projects, nor his vacillating decision-making process. Preventive detention, rather than the dilution of the electoral process or the arbitrary dismissal of ministers, was highlighted as the cornerstone of his dictatorialism. Even his economic advisers tried to persuade him that the arrest without trial of prominent members of society was detrimental to economic confidence. Although local managerial talent may have been scared away, international capital was wholly hypocritical in its attitude to strong-arm political tactics and it is an open question whether foreign vilification was as harmful to national progress as articulate intellectuals supposed.

In domestic politics internment was a slippery slope down which Nkrumah was the first to launch himself but down which others were to follow. Slowly the use of detention spread from prospective saboteurs and assassins to legitimate critics. The most serious case, which did Nkrumah's reputation untold harm, concerned the great national leader, Dr. J. B. Danquah, who was incarcerated in the specially built security prison of Nsawam. Despite age, infirmity, and eventually illness, Nkrumah refused to contemplate his release and eventually Danquah died in prison in 1965. His death was seen as parricidal by many who considered Danquah the father of the nation, and Nkrumah his wayward son. Members of the legitimate opposition began to restrict their opinions to private conversation and later took the road to exile.

The misuse of internment gradually spread from the political heartland to the provinces. Detention became a means whereby local political bosses could settle old scores and obtain private advantage. The supervision of extra-judicial arrests was never adequate. People could be arrested by jealous rivals who wanted their political office, their business assets, or even their wives and mistresses. The scale of arrests was never large by the prewar standards of Europe, but by 1966 a thousand people were in prison either as security risks or as a result of feuding between local power barons. In a small country many people were embittered by having a friend, relative, or colleague who had had a taste of prison.

By the time political detention had got out of hand, Nkrumah had become a partial recluse in his fortified government offices. His fear of assassination modified his political behavior and prevented him from recharging his batteries in the political arena. The country spiraled downward but sycophants feared to tell him the truth. The health services deteriorated dangerously but no one dared admit to the president that the country had run out of pharmaceutical drugs. Imported food, a major feature of urban life, disappeared from the shops in a situation explosively similar to January 1948 but protest was equated with subversion. A free society felt itself no longer to be free. Objectively there may have been more freedom in Ghana in the 1960s than in the majority of the world's nations, but compared to the heady days of the 1950s people felt oppressed, disappointed, and ready for a change. The leader they had worshipped had become remote and unhearing. The great problem of independent Africa was how to find a new savior. They were ready to come out on the streets and follow another leader. Nobody would have predicted that the change might come from the despised police force.

The unpopularity of preventive detention was not confined to those who suffered arrest. It was also unpopular with those who were responsible for carrying out the arrests. The reasons why the police took part in the overthrow of Nkrumah had much to do with their own internal ambitions, and their relations with the army, but their growing unpopularity was one factor. Unpopularity was not new, since the police had been the agents of repression under colonial rule, nor was it wholly undeserved, since corrupt practices had spread in the service and private payments were imposed on both real and alleged lawbreakers. For the police to further jeopardize their position by carrying out unpopular arrests accentuated their politicization. The crisis of the police force was brought to a head when a member of the presidential guard attempted to murder Nkrumah in the grounds of his own home. Nkrumah, the hitherto charismatic and open leader who thrived on crowd appeal, found his public life further curtailed and his style becoming more autocratic. The police, on the other hand, found that their responsibilities and resources were being taken away from them and given to new security units. Like the unions and the market women they began to wonder about the need for change. The police, moreover, had access to modern systems of transport and communications which reached into the remotest corners of the country. It was ironic, in the light of police activity in European police-states, that the Ghana police could present themselves as the saviors of democracy when the time came to topple Nkrumah.

The Army

The biggest problem which President Nkrumah faced once the last governor-general, the eminent British statesman the Earl of Listowel, had left the country, was the problem of a national army. He was probably not aware that this was to be his most difficult political task. Neither he nor any of his advisers thought it likely that it would be from the army that the real challenge to his authority would come. Nkrumah did not worry about how to keep the army satisfied but rather how to give them real teeth with which to carry out his pan-continental policy of liberation and unification. He decided that he would need an increased army, a modern air force, and an ocean-going navy. He gave the task of building up the services to a British major-general, H. T. Alexander, who recorded his experiences in a sympathetic but lucidly critical memoir. Nkrumah, like most civilian political liberals, had no concept of the real cost of an armed force. Modern nations, he argued, had armies, jet-fighters, and frigates so of course the new Africa must seek the same military standards. But Nkrumah's "New Africa" still consisted only of Ghana, a farming nation with only about 4 percent of the wealth of Britain or France and a limited literate manpower available for military training. A program of militarization was nevertheless set up which was epitomized by extravagance in equipment and short-cuts in training. The extravagance involved the purchase of small but not practically useful warships to be stationed at a naval base in Guggisberg's great harbor at Takoradi. It also involved the planning of an air force base, initially at Takoradi also, but later to be transferred to the northern town of Tamale and equipped with aircraft of dubious operational value. But the greatest problem arose not from the burden which this equipment put on the exchequer but from the problem of training new men.

General Alexander estimated that in 1960 Ghana's schools were producing seven hundred boys per annum who could usefully be accepted into the armed forces and that the maximum that the army could expect to ask for was one hundred of these. He also thought that within five years it would be possible to train and expand an officer corps with the experience to take over completely from the British expatriates who provided a part of the senior training and command personnel in the Ghana armed forces. Nkrumah wanted to move faster than that. He therefore planned to deplete the immediate cohort of senior school-leavers of no less than four hundred of their number for military training. Since British training was slow, meticulous, and expensive, he was tempted by the suggestion that military training could be done more cheaply and rapidly in the Soviet Union. Within two years he decided to dispense with all British officers, including the chief of defense staff himself. Promotions became rapid, thus creating great expectations in the army hierarchy. Training became split between the old guard of British-style officers and the prospective new guard of Soviet-trained men. Expectation and rivalry created problems that were to be serious, as the outgoing commander had predicted. He even hinted, with a perspicacity which Nkrumah himself was unable to grasp, that rapid promotion and a split military tradition might be fatal to the regime that the army was designed to serve. Such proved to be the case.

The Fall of Nkrumah

One of the big questions about the fall of Nkrumah is whether there was any foreign involvement in his overthrow. In the generation after 1966 "destabilization" became a recognized concept as governments in "the North" took a hand in pulling down — or propping up — governments in "the South" to suit their own interests. Overt interventions in Africa came from France and South Africa, but Britain and the Soviet Union were also active, notably in Nigeria. American policy was sometimes covert though the attempted destabilization of Angola in 1975 took place in a blaze of world publicity. In Ghana the question of foreign involvement in ending the Nkrumah era was complex. Nkrumah seems to have been surprised that Americans took personal umbrage at his analysis of their activities in his book *Neo-Colonialism: The Last Stage of Imperialism* and he was disappointed that as a consequence Jacqueline Kennedy was dissuaded from attending the inauguration of the Volta dam. Soon afterwards he persuaded himself that America had taken a hand in fostering the coup that overthrew him. Contemporary research, for instance by Ruth First in *The*

Barrel of a Gun, showed no conclusive evidence of foreign intrigue, though the West clearly thought it had squeezed all that was possible from Nkrumah and moved with alacrity to exploit his overthrow and befriend his armed successors.[7] The ten agents of the American Central Intelligence Agency who were stationed in Accra in 1966 would, however, have been improbably inept if they had not been in touch with the plotters and they may conceivably have helped to fund them. But, as President Johnson's spokesman put it, the CIA "did not throw the match into the haystack."

Ghana was a prisoner of the West in every way at the time of the 1966 coup. Falling cocoa prices were not manipulated, as some liked to believe, to bankrupt Nkrumah's government, but the decline was a factor behind the coup. Efforts to find alternative markets in the Soviet bloc had proved disastrous, with cocoa sold to Russia turning up on the London commodity market to provide the Soviet Union with hard currency and to undercut the price of direct sales from Africa. Two days before the coup the price paid to cocoa farmers was again reduced in a profoundly unpopular budget move. This was in line with policy advocated by the International Monetary Fund, though the fund was concerned with orthodoxy, loyalty to the West, and the reduction of government influence and not with radical innovation. The obverse of the failing commodity prices was the hard-sell strategy of industrial salesmen who continued to encourage Ghana to build up a debt beyond that which the economy could service. Terms of trade were running against all Third World countries, yet Britain guaranteed Ghana credits for a wholly ill-conceived project to build a shipyard at a time when ships could not be sold even at give-away prices. At the same time a West German firm advanced credits of no less than £60 million to make Ghana hostage to the German export drive.

Trade was not the only field in which Nkrumah found his relationship with the powers difficult. He also confronted them in two strategic matters. The first concerned the proposed establishment of a small Soviet air base in the north of Ghana which might be used by Cuba and other eastern satellites in spreading their military influence. This threat to Western hegemony was compounded by alleged assistance from East Germany in improving the Ghana intelligence services. The second strategic issue of Nkrumah's last months concerned the white rebellion in Rhodesia. Nkrumah bitterly condemned Britain's Labour prime minister, Harold Wilson, for failing to take military action. As the champion of African freedom Nkrumah considered taking action himself. Such a bold prospect sounded his death knell. The Ghanaian army, fearful that Nkrumah might offer to free Zimbabwe from its white settlers by armed force, decided that the time had come for him to be removed. The army, in cooperation with the police, and to the acclaim of the cocoa farmers, the trade unionists, the market women, the intellectuals, the bureaucrats, and the regional chiefs, mounted their coup on 24 February 1966. It was in his capacity as the hero of Africa that Nkrumah finally overstretched himself and fell.

4

African Hero

At dawn on 24 February 1966 an armored column which had driven through the night seized the residence of Kwame Nkrumah during his absence and declared over the radio that the president had been deposed. Nkrumah spent six sad years crying in the wilderness before dying of cancer in a lonely Romanian hospital bed. Thereafter his reputation began slowly to be reassessed. His career took on a new perspective in resurgent black America where his student roots had been. He was looked at in a new light in Britain which had given him his first opportunity in politics. Nkrumah took on a fresh meaning in the Soviet bloc which had been so inept in its efforts to support him. But above all Nkrumah's place in history was looked at anew in Africa. He had been the African patriot *par excellence,* though Africa had been slow to understand his message about the neocolonial sequel to independence and had firmly turned its back on his preaching of unity.

Nkrumah's thinking on how to establish African unity had gone through four phases. The first was a direct sequel to the Manchester conference of 1945. Nkrumah and other like-minded leaders convened a series of conferences to discuss the strategies for economic cooperation and political integration. Secondly, Nkrumah confronted the realities of the new French "empire" in Africa that was being built by Charles de Gaulle in total contradiction to his own ideas of African harmonization across the old colonial borders. Thirdly, Nkrumah had to come to terms with the advent of the super-powers in black Africa, particularly in the ex-Belgian Congo. It was here that he gained his first experience of the role of the military in politics. Fourthly, and lastly, Nkrumah had to confront the realities of entrenched white power in the southern quarter of the continent. The war of liberation began in 1961, in Angola, but it was the unilateral declaration of independence by the white Rhodesians of Zimbabwe that brought Nkrumah into contact with the front line.

After the world re-appraisal, and the African re-evaluation, it was the turn of Ghana to look back on its erstwhile savior and measure his achievements and failures in the historical spectrum. It did so in the chastening light of his successors' experiences. Ghanaians discovered that Nkrumah, who had been so bitterly denounced for failing to match up to the expectations that he had aroused, had faced problems which were generic rather than personal. His weaknesses were no greater than those of his contemporaries or rivals, but he had been the first to face the storms of statesmanship and there had been few navigational aids. Nkrumah came to be remembered as the bold visionary, the man of urgency and purpose. Academics who had once derided their president told David Rooney, Nkrumah's most thorough biographer, that their charismatic leader who was wooed by East and West, had been "a man with an inspiring, confident, and comprehensive philosophy." Nkrumah could lie easy in his new grave on home soil.[8]

The World Stage

Twenty years after his fall the name Nkrumah could still bring a quickening of the pulse to black people around the world. The slogan "black is beautiful" had not yet gained currency but Nkrumah had given people a pride in their black skins and a confidence in themselves which slavery and colonialism had eroded. A black prime minister visiting the United States in 1952 was something utterly new when black America was still in the grip of segregation and the Alabama bus boycotts had not even begun. It took America another twelve years to give even legal equality to blacks through the Civil Rights Act of 1964. That was still a long way from political power. Afro-Americans began to visit Ghana to taste freedom while their own campaign was stalled. Some radical blacks talked of "returning" to Africa, as Marcus Garvey had done, but the idea did not catch on and those that came were often ill at ease. They found themselves welcomed as "white men" rather than as soul brothers. A couple of hundred black Americans nevertheless worked in Ghana escaping from the realities of American prejudice and discrimination and seeking new black heroes. Maya Angelou was among these trans-Atlantic émigrés who admired Nkrumah to the point of adulation though most never met him.

Nkrumah gave an official welcome to very diverse leaders of the black movement in America, starting with the old folk hero Louis Armstrong. The Christian directors of the civil rights movement kept in touch, and the Reverend Martin Luther King was the nearest equivalent to an American Nkrumah. Du Bois, the old advocate of Pan-Africanism, emigrated to Ghana at Nkrumah's invitation and died there at the age of ninety-six, symbolically enough on the very day of the great civil rights march in Washington. The more radical blacks, Malcolm X, Stokely Carmichael, the Black Muslims, also came to see the dream nation. But few felt at ease in the unexpected poverty of West Africa. Their ideals of equality and fraternity became uncomfortably unrealistic in a country materially poorer than the poorest of American ghettos. Those who stayed chose guiltily to live in the expatriate style of the

Ghana middle class with tiled roofs, piped water, nightly sanitation services, and tropical flower gardens. They were separated from "the people" by an uncomfortable gulf. The Ghana bourgeoisie felt uncomfortable with the "Nkrumah groupies" who embarrassingly sang the unstinted praises of the "redeemer" without questioning what happened beneath the surface. Black Americans came to be suspected by Ghanaians as potential fifth-columnists, the masked agents of American ideology. When attempts were made on Nkrumah's life patriotic Ghanaians sought scapegoats. They did not look to the British, the old imperial rulers who in some curious way were still covertly admired and exempted from xenophobic attack. They suspected instead the new arrivals with their mixed loyalties and crossed signals and wondered whether American intelligence services hired Afro-Americans. Black émigrés found that hero worship was safer from a distance and slipped away, back to the certainties of America.

The reverse side of the Afro-American image of Nkrumah the hero was the white American portrait of Nkrumah the bogeyman. In truth, as has been demonstrated, America gained enormously from the Nkrumah years. It learned invaluable lessons in how to manipulate Third World politicians and extract colonial wealth through neocolonial structures. Nkrumah's complex love-hate relationship with America provided the United States with its first entrée into independent Africa. This entrée was followed up not only in conservative Zaire and Kenya, but also in left-leaning Guinea and Egypt, and most surprisingly of all in the Soviet satellite of Angola where America controlled the oil industry in partnership with the fiercely hostile local political élite. America had well and truly learned to sup with the devil, casting Nkrumah in the role of first devil. While Ghana was being milked, its leader was being denigrated as a socialist who would nationalize assets without compensation, as a dictator who would crush his opponents without mercy, as an opportunist who would accumulate wealth for himself and his cronies in the most blatantly corrupt fashion. The media which had once thrived on the success of the world's first democratic black leader now thrived on denigrating him as he wriggled on the hook which had been baited for him. The victim was being blamed for his own predicament by his oppressor in time-honored style. Under such pressure Nkrumah found his energy and self-confidence beginning to desert him. By 1966 he was exhausted. He had been in power for fifteen years, about twice as long as Western democracies normally allow to their leaders.

Nkrumah's relations with Britain and the British were as complex as those of an adolescent son. His admiration and emulation were tempered with impassioned criticism. He profoundly believed in British institutions, but was enraged when they failed to work for him, whether in his parliament or in the judiciary or in the security services. He was ambivalent about the value of American education, despite his own training, and preferred British forms and standards. His friendship with the royal family was genuine, he had been a guest at Balmoral, and had accepted membership of the Privy Council since formal British titles were not available in Commonwealth republics. He chose British designs in engineering and construction when they were available, even down to the color of the road signs. On the reverse side Britain's admiration for Nkrumah was less fulsome. The British were riled by his moral preaching on international issues, especially when they suspected themselves of being in the wrong, as over the Rhodesian rebellion. The British press also failed to understand the nearly schizophrenic distinction between Nkrumah's anti-imperial rhetoric and his profound attachment to most things British. British expatriates who worked in Ghana noted the intemperate cynicism towards Nkrumah which pervaded governments of either hue at Westminster and were disquieted by the audible sigh of official relief when Nkrumah fell.

The third external power in Ghana was the Soviet Union, which was even more inexperienced than the United States when it entered African politics after the war. Moscow wanted to bring succor to the nationalists of Africa and so cut away the colonial support for Western capitalism. It was apparently not sensitive to the thought that Soviet assistance might be the kiss of death to Nkrumah. More bluntly the Soviet Union was anxious to replenish its own war-drained coffers by replacing Britain as Africa's trading partner. It soon ran up against old cultural preferences even more starkly than America had done. Soviet manufactured goods were unacceptable to a market very sensitive to price and quality. Attempts to institute barter deals led to profound public antagonism and a realization that Russia was not a country with which lightly to do business. It was in the field of military training and weaponry that the Soviet Union gained a small toehold. This toehold was to be fatal to Nkrumah whose army was steeped in Sandhurst conservatism. It was also a disaster in the eyes of public opinion. To the average Ghanaian seven thousand British expatriates were a normal and unthreatening part of the landscape. The two hundred Russians in the country, on the other hand, were seen as a foreign threat. The police and the army felt in particular that their access to national resources was liable to be threatened by new Russian-trained paramilitary and security units. Soviet friendship may not have triggered a rival foreign intervention, but it did trigger a self-interested military *coup d'état*. The Soviet Union, as Padmore had warned, had not yet understood Nkrumah or Africa. Worse still it did not help Nkrumah's crusade for African unity but played the neocolonial game of divide and rule along with the best of them.

Pan-Africanism

No sooner had Nkrumah won independence for Ghana than he introduced the Pan-African spirit of the Manchester conference to Africa.

Henceforth this was to be a central preoccupation. In April 1958 he convened a meeting of independent African states at Accra. The eight participants could not have been more diverse. Ethiopia was a conservative medieval empire governed by an ethnic aristocracy of Semitic Christian warlords who were slowly recovering from seven years of fascist overrule by Italy. Liberia was an oligarchic client of the United States with a proud black tradition but little understanding of the mass stirrings of African nationalism. Egypt was a new friend of the Soviet Union ruled by radical soldiers who had recently routed the monarchy, the Muslims, and the British. Morocco and Libya were Islamic kingdoms with significant populations of Christian settlers from Europe. Tunisia and Sudan were democratic republics with strong traditions of French and British colonial élitism. Not one of them was at all close to the liberation ideology of Nkrumah, and yet they met together, committed themselves to the decolonization of Africa by nonviolent means, and agreed to condone the armed struggle in Algeria and South Africa. They resolved not to interfere in each others' internal affairs.

Nkrumah's second attempt to bring home to Africa the ideal of Pan-Africanism was conducted on a much wider and more popular basis. He convened a conference of all African peoples in December 1958. This conference projected an unexpectedly rapid agenda for decolonization. It was not a conference for those comfortable leaders who already held power, but one for the hungry young radicals who thirsted after power. Ambitious but little-known young men made their way to Accra to meet like-minded political novices from other colonies. For the first time they could see what independence meant in Africa, they could dream of liberation as a proximate reality, they could feel the pulse of a whole continent. Nkrumah had every right to be proud of the vision he had instilled and to be optimistic about the future. Within months of the conference local leaders such as

Lumumba of Zaire, Mboya of Kenya, and Kaunda of Zambia had become African idols.

Nkrumah's All-African People's Conference gave heart to individual national leaders, but did not significantly advance the cause of African unity. The new statesmen were very divided on the question of cooperation after independence. The radicals met in one camp and the conservatives in another. Some advocated regional integration while others denounced them as saboteurs of the grand Pan-African design. Some supported economic collaboration while others preferred to seek constitutional links. A few were prepared to relinquish their hard-won freedom for the greater good of the whole continent, but most were jealous of their new presidential status. Many were grudging in their gratitude to Nkrumah for his visionary initiative and fearful that he would steal their limelight in any transcontinental government.

In May 1963 the new nations of Africa finally met together in Ethiopia to patch up a compromise and to found an Organization of African Unity. The program was to be a minimal one, and even in relation to the liberation of South Africa several members were subsequently to break rank and engage in dialogue and trade. But right from the start the leaders firmly rejected Nkrumah's thesis that the territories partitioned in the "Scramble for Africa" were too small to be viable nations on a world stage and should therefore unite. The policy of unraveling colonial boundaries which appeared economically logical in the 1940s looked utopian in the 1960s. A common market for Africa now seemed even more difficult to achieve than a common market for Europe.

Nkrumah did not abandon hope, but in 1965 invited the heads of state to a glittering banquet. It was to be his last throw as the self-appointed leader of Africa. The hospitality was lavish and the purpose-built conference center exhausted the resources of a small cocoa republic with a dwindling income and a rising debt. The outcome was disastrous. At a domestic level belt-tightening Ghanaians saw money squandered on fleets of plush cars for VIP guests when they themselves were hard pressed to find yams in the food market let alone batteries for their flashlights or kerosene for their refrigerators. Prestige as the premier nation in Africa did appeal to the Ghanaian national sense of pride, but the cost had now outweighed the benefit. More seriously still, the achievements of the national leader were called into question despite strident propaganda in government newspapers. African unity was rejected again. Nkrumah was seen to be a failure, even a naïve fool, in the international arena. His days were numbered.

Charles de Gaulle and Africa

The rejection of African unity had as much to do with the rise of a new European interest in Africa as with the parochial preoccupations of the first generation of nationalist heads of state. In particular France was able to build an entirely new type of empire in its previously much neglected African colonies. The initiative came from General de Gaulle who became Nkrumah's most powerful and successful rival on the African stage. Their two careers ran in exact parallel from war-time exile in the 1940s, to unexpected power in the 1950s, to humiliating rejection in the 1960s. But whereas Nkrumah was remembered as the proponent of an unrealized united states of Africa, de Gaulle's empire in Africa weathered the upheavals of 1968 and became his posthumous monument for the next generation.

While Nkrumah was in exile in America preaching to black congregations and organizing cells of African students, de Gaulle was in exile in Britain, organizing refugees, claiming leadership of the French resistance, broadcasting to the occupied territories of France and the empire, badgering Anglo-Saxons to invade Morocco and Madagascar. He persuaded a handful of settlers and administrators in Brazzaville, in the

French Congo, to support his "Free France" movement. In a masterly stroke he appointed a black West Indian, Felix Eboué, as his governor-general over all the territories of equatorial Africa. Although nominally colonial, French Equatorial Africa was cut off from occupied France and Eboué became a quasi-autonomous black leader, the contemporary of Tubman and Haile Selassie. Free French colonial ideology was explicitly assimilationist in regard to the tiny colonial élite, and diametrically opposed to the racism in the Vichy colonies of West Africa. Assimilation was also more openly advocated than in British West Africa where a lingering racism still hobbled the educated élite of urban society.

De Gaulle did not survive long in politics at the end of the war but, little more than a decade later, he returned to power in Paris as an executive president with wide civil and military powers and a mandate to find a viable future for the French Empire after the fiasco of Vietnam in 1954 and a costly military stalemate in Algeria. De Gaulle faced the prospect that Nkrumah and the British might initiate a wholesale decolonization of tropical Africa, a policy which he set about arresting. His first strategy was to break French Africa up into small pieces, each of which could be more easily dealt with in an unequal partnership. Nkrumah spoke out passionately against this "balkanization" of Africa. He found that instead of negotiating with a single set of Francophone African leaders, as he had been doing since 1945, he now had to deal with fourteen sets of politicians each with newly enhanced prestige and a commitment to the status that they had been accorded by de Gaulle.

De Gaulle's policy in Africa was one of stick and carrot, which commanded resources which Nkrumah could not hope to match. The carrot consisted of integration into a French "community" with economic inducements to retain the colonial nexus. The stick became evident when one territory, Guinea, under the leadership of a trade unionist quite unlike the assimilated black citizens who ran the other

French colonies, turned down de Gaulle's gilded offer of a semi-independent form of self-government in close association with France. The mailed fist was hard, and France withdrew from Guinea in 1958, ripping out telephones, expropriating government files, withdrawing personnel, cutting off trade, and generally trying to ensure that a country which said *"non"* to de Gaulle would be incapable of survival.

Nkrumah was the first to respond to the French assault on Guinea. Regardless of his limited national resources he bailed Guinea out in a rash but magnificent display of African solidarity. His price was the initiation of West African unification through a Ghana-Guinea union. The proposal was a difficult one to sustain since the two countries had no common border, no common language, no common traditions of administration, of defense, of policing, or of foreign relations. The harmonization of colonial systems was later to prove well nigh impossible even in the much more straightforward unification of the two Camerouns. The Ghana-Guinea union was magnanimous, ambitious, and unrealistic. It also had a profound effect on the struggle between Nkrumah and de Gaulle over the future shape of West Africa.

One immediate consequence of Nkrumah's support for the bankrupted state of Guinea was the advent of the Soviet Union in West Africa. Although very short of finance and technology, and very limited in political intelligence and colonial experience, Russia did help Nkrumah keep Guinea afloat and so forced de Gaulle significantly to improve the offer that it was willing to make to the other French colonies. The "no" had succeeded in the short run, and francophone politicians could no longer afford to appear to accept a freedom that was any less complete than that of Ghana or Guinea. Nkrumah thus drove de Gaulle to a second round of constitutional bargaining in which the French maestro perfected his strategy of neocolonial "partnership."

The 1960 round of decolonization offered each French territory full independence, later known disparagingly as "flag independence," a president, an anthem, a parliament, a capital city, and a team of "advisers." What the new countries did not get was a currency of their own. The renamed French colonial franc, controlled from Paris, was to be the basis of all internal and external finance. France was to retain almost monopolistic trading rights even when Common Market regulations gave theoretical access to other European manufacturing nations. De Gaulle thus bought out all his African leaders, save one, and isolated Nkrumah with three hostile neighbors controlled by Gaullist advisers, intelligence officers, and when necessary paratroops. The Gaullist solution was such a success that only one of the new leaders — in Gabon — had to be put back on his pedestal by military intervention. But Nkrumah did not give up his struggle with France.

One mild hiccup in de Gaulle's plan seemed to give Nkrumah an opportunity to peel Mali off the French grand design and annex it to his Pan-African cause. But Timbuktu and the Niger towns were a long way up a rutted track used mainly by salt lorries or cattle drovers and the two countries had no common border. France did not over-react to the proposal to attach Mali to the ephemeral Ghana-Guinea union but waited for the moment to pass. Soon it found that it could work profitably with regimes of any political coloring and when some ex-French colonies chose Marxist leaders cooperation with Paris carried on almost unruffled by the tone of the nationalist rhetoric.

France's arrogance in Africa was symbolized by de Gaulle's decision to build his own nuclear weapons and to use Africa to test them. The British campaign for nuclear disarmament allied itself with Nkrumah to draw attention to such disdain for human and ecological rights in Africa. The bombs were tested regardless, with unknown consequences but with no outcry from the neocolonial puppets. De Gaulle felt sufficiently confident to end the long colonial war in Algeria and create a client state in North Africa too. A cease-fire was achieved despite settler hysteria, and although political relations with Algeria were cool, Saharan oil and gas flowed to France without interruption. Nkrumah, the long-term champion of Algerian liberation, had been outmaneuvered again.

The Congo Crisis

Guinea had presented Nkrumah with his first opportunity to act out his role as leader of the continent. It also taught him to appreciate how limited his financial resources were, how fickle friendship with the Soviet Union could be, and how powerful the French sway in Africa was. His second opportunity to take on a leadership role for the whole continent occurred two years later in the former Belgian Congo, later Zaire. This time the scenario was quite different, his potential ally was the United States, and his opponent was Belgium, a less formidable metropolitan enemy than France.

The Congo crisis broke in July 1960, in the first days of independence. The army mutinied when it discovered how little change independence brought. Belgium invaded to protect its citizens. Lumumba, the new prime minister, appealed to the United Nations for military assistance both in repelling the Belgians and in disarming his own troops. Nkrumah offered the United Nations the services of his army. He was anxious to defend newly won freedom, but also perhaps to form an alliance with the Congo which would be a firmer basis for African unity than his union with the crippled Guinea.

The Ghana venture in Congo began with bizarre bravado, as its commander portrayed with dry humor in his autobiography. Nkrumah offered to send his general and twenty-five soldiers to Kinshasa, then called Léopoldville, to stop the molesting of civilians, to persuade the Congo army to return to barracks, and to replace the expeditionary force of Belgian paratroops. Nkrumah had neither a radio network able to communicate with Kinshasa nor a transport plane capable of crossing the Gulf of Guinea. His inventive commander-in-chief managed, however, to borrow a Royal Air Force Comet which happened to be visiting Accra airport and persuaded the British government to allow him to fly it to the Congo. On arrival the Belgians were astonished to find that the commander of the unwelcome Ghanaian soldiers was a British general. Unfortunately General Alexander spoke no French so, almost unbelievably, he recruited an American journalist to interpret Nkrumah's message to the mutinous soldiers. Equally bizarre was his decision to avoid the British embassy, as being too closely linked with imperialism, and to seek logistic support from the American embassy. The idea that America was neutral in the decolonization conflict may appear naïve with hindsight, but in 1960 the United States, which had sided with Egypt at Suez against France and Britain, was still the champion of freedom. Only during the course of the Congo conflict did America come to be widely identified with imperial-type interests of its own in Africa. But the American embassy was only a slight ally for Nkrumah's advance guard and Alexander had to seek more substantial support.[9]

In a second personal initiative Nkrumah's commander borrowed a plane to fly up the river in search of the Congo prime minister, Patrice Lumumba. At Kinsangani, Stanleyville, a British tobacco manufacturer provided him with an expatriate view of the local political scene. He finally made contact with the prime minister and at last gained a veneer of political legitimacy for the Ghanaian presence. Thereafter the mutineers were gradually calmed, the United Nations force took on a more formal shape and command structure, the domestic interests began to square up for a civil war, and international powers sought to clarify their future interests in the heart of Africa. Nkrumah's solo effort had been a mixture of bravery, idealism, and farce. The remainder of the

Congo story was violence and tragedy. The Ghana army emerged from it indelibly marked.

Throughout the Congo campaign Nkrumah supported the United Nations more or less loyally but learned how slow and frustrating it was to conduct policy through an organization built on complex checks and balances in which small nations had little influence. His army, meanwhile, learned that in other countries, Sandhurst rules notwithstanding, soldiers played a commanding role in politics. They also learned that trying to influence the civil wars of other nations could be brutal and cost lives. They emerged from the Congo very anxious not to get involved in another "peace-keeping" operation let alone in a campaign of their own. Hence their horror in 1965 when they suspected that Nkrumah might be planning to tarnish their Sam Brownes with a rash foray into the Rhodesian veldt.

Southern Africa

In seeking a heroic role as the African savior, Nkrumah might have expected to receive the broadest support over freeing southern Africa from white domination. A first step was taken by campaigning to have the "mandate" to rule Namibia withdrawn from South Africa. But despite United Nations resolutions, South Africa refused to quit and Namibian decolonization was delayed for a generation. Nkrumah also took a lead in trying to persuade the world community that Portugal should be invited to transfer power over its colonies to national leaders. In particular he pointed out to the International Labour Organization that Portugal still used forced labor for economic and not merely for punitive ends. No heed was taken and in 1961 rebellion broke out in Angola. A moral stance was not enough to carry weight in the world of realpolitik. The otherwise liberal President Kennedy actually reversed his policy of "Africa for the Africans" when Portugal threatened to close his Atlantic air bases and so threaten the lifeline between America and Israel so dear to Jewish voters. America went further in Angola, however, and decided that perhaps a friendly colonial umbrella provided by anti-Communist Portugal might give United States business better access to Africa than the fickle black government of a national bourgeoisie with strange loyalties to its former colonial masters. Kennedy discreetly allowed the Portuguese not only to renew their tenancy of the African colonies, but even to use NATO military supplies for their colonial war. The liberation committee of the Organization of African Unity, the one organ of hope in Nkrumah's Pan-African vision, lost not only the Namibian round, but also the Angolan one. While Kennedy's Peace Corps poured into Nkrumah's Ghana, his guns pounded the front line where black Africa was trying to challenge white Africa.

The fiercest confrontation between white and black Africa occurred in Zimbabwe. This was where Nkrumah met his ultimate challenge. In the 1950s Zimbabwe was administered by a self-governing regime of white Rhodesians. The black population, helped by the newly invented transistor radio, followed the career of Nkrumah with close interest and expected that full democracy would be granted to Zimbabwe as it had been to all other British colonies within the tropics. In 1965, however, local settler politicians decreed otherwise and rebelled against the British crown by unilaterally declaring the country an independent white state. All previous rebellions in Africa had met with instant armed retribution by Britain. Nkrumah naturally assumed that the United Kingdom's Labour government would immediately send troops to quash the racist revolt. It did not do so. Nkrumah, a lifelong admirer of Britain, was painfully disillusioned.

When the government of Harold Wilson refused to invade Rhodesia and arrest the rebel leader, Ian Smith, Nkrumah could only believe that it was out of an unwillingness to treat white dissidents in the same way that black colonial dissidents had always been treated. To some extent Nkrumah was right in his diagnosis of racism. In particular the British army had close personal links with the army of Rhodesia and could not be relied upon to fight "kith and kin" in the way that it had fought Kenya's freedom fighters a decade earlier. Nkrumah decided that Africa itself must take responsibility for ridding Zimbabwe of its cowboy regime. He seemed to have little recognition of the fact that the Wilson government had real logistic problems in ending the rebellion, and not merely racist inhibitions. When Nkrumah talked of preparing his army for a new Congo-type operation he caused dismay. The prospect of being sent to war against a well-armed, well-trained, white army three thousand miles from home was too much for Ghana's soldiers. They rebelled against Nkrumah before their skins could be suicidally put at risk. Pan-African idealism brought Nkrumah's final ruin.

If Zimbabwe provided one cause of Nkrumah's downfall, the occasion was supplied by another of his visionary endeavors. In 1966 the United States and the Soviet Union were settling into their second vicarious round of Cold War fighting on Third World soil, this time in Vietnam. Nkrumah's commitment to the non-aligned movement established in Indonesia in 1955 led him to seek ways of driving out the super-powers and restoring peace to the innocent victims of the conflict. In February 1966 Nkrumah set off for the Far East, regardless of extravagance or of the critical situation he left at home, to offer his impartial services as an arbiter in Vietnam. He called first at Beijing where Zhou en Lai, who had recently been in Ghana and knew the tense situation there, was given the unhappy task of informing Nkrumah that he was no longer president. Nkrumah had finally overstretched himself and his army and police had wisely chosen to strike a coup in furtherance of their own ends while the master was out of the country.

The model for the Ghana *coup d'état* came from Nigeria and it was perhaps significant that Nigeria should have been indirectly involved in Nkrumah's final failure. The slow political awakening of Africa's giant nation inevitably cast a shadow over Ghana's leader. Under the British, Nigeria had been partitioned three ways, and resolving the tensions between three sub-national identities absorbed the country's political energies. Despite this inward preoccupation Nigerian politicians, including President Azikiwe, who during his self-imposed Gold Coast exile had been a father figure to the young Nkrumah, could not allow their small radical neighbor to set the international agenda. Indeed, when the leader of the Nigerian opposition supported Nkrumah's call for African unity he was locked away for subversion. The heavyweights of Nigerian politics were aristocratic Muslims from the north with no appetite for Nkrumah's visionary radicalism. Like him, however, they never suspected that a British-trained army might interfere in political affairs, and when the Nigerian army did so, in January 1966, English-speaking Africans everywhere were shocked. Nigeria had always been a more violent colony than Ghana, but military intervention was seen as "Latin" behavior, recognizable in Spanish America, or at a pinch in French Africa. It was not to be expected in Commonwealth Africa. In Ghana the political and bureaucratic class, supporters and opponents of Nkrumah alike, were profoundly surprised. The military, however, took the hint with alacrity. Their Ghana coup came within weeks of the Nigerian one. In both countries the coup leaders were men with Congo experience.

The Nkrumah Heritage

The rehabilitation of Nkrumah as Africa's hero began with the recognition that "neocolonialism" was a real power that enthralled Africa. The campaign of denigration that the West had launched against Nkrumah concentrated on making out that neocolonialism was a figment of his imagination. By the 1970s it was clear that the neocolonial forcing of political choices in Africa was a reality. Blaming the ills of the new African regimes on the iniquities of the colonial past was no longer a credible alibi for failure. It was the need to understand the financial influences which held Africa in thrall as a producer of underpriced raw materials and a consumer of over-priced foreign manufactures which brought Nkrumah's style of analysis to the fore. The predicament was well understood by Nkrumah's East African contemporary, Julius Nyerere, as he watched helplessly while the price of sisal fell and the price of tractors to cultivate it rose. The trap was made deeper as individual industrial nations clubbed together to control price mechanisms in Africa. The most pervasive of the conventions, signed periodically in Lomé just outside Ghana's borders, guaranteed — in exchange for concessions chosen by Europe — that individual African countries would keep the industrial nations of the north supplied with cheap raw materials rather than cooperate in setting up processing and manufacturing plants of their own in the ideal manner of which Nkrumah dreamed. The Lomé scenario would have exceeded his worst nightmares and his stature began to be reassessed.

One form of foreign control, the corrupting of politicians, proved particularly difficult to eradicate and even when state presidents did not themselves accept payment to influence their decisions, they often found it expedient to allow financial malpractice among their associates as a method of control through threat of exposure. Nkrumah, although able to analyze the predicament caused by corruption, was no better able to escape from it than his contemporaries. Another form of foreign control affected the armies of Africa whose officers modeled themselves on colonial practice and relied for weapons on strategic partnerships. Foreign influence could and did both trigger military coups and stop military coups. France stopped a military coup in Gabon to preserve its oil and uranium resources, and America stopped one in Kenya to protect its Indian Ocean bases, but neither was inclined to stop a military coup against Nkrumah. Indeed the West might have promoted Nkrumah's overthrow, as it had planned to overthrow Lumumba, had local initiative not been taken.

The essence of neocolonialism was not only economic domination, business corruption, and military destabilization, but also control by pervasive cultural influence. A later generation came to recognize that the most difficult aspect of decolonization was the decolonization of the mind. Banking, insurance, transport, and investment were the public core of preferred managerial continuity. Education, fashion, religion, and cinema were the personal manifestations of cultural choice. Nkrumah spoke eloquently about the African personality, but life in Africa was changing, more people lived in tin shanties than in thatched houses, and modernization was associated with welcome changes from abroad. Nkrumah reveled in national costumes, but his contemporaries felt more dignified in jackets and ties. Only in one field, music, did Africa radiate its culture out to the world rather than absorb the homogenized cosmopolitan culture influences of others. The powerful, innovative bands of Ghana, using modern instruments, amplifiers, and recording equipment, were a cultural manifestation that carried African *joie de vivre* to Europe and beyond in one significant reverse of the tide of neocolonial culture.

It was not only abroad that Nkrumah's reputation underwent reappraisal. While in office Nkrumah had been regularly accused of personal financial corruption. The case was far from proven and although his finances were unorthodox, and funds were channeled to causes he held dear by means that auditors could not approve, Nkrumah did not accumulate a large private fortune in the manner of some other African heads of state. His years of exile in Guinea were spent writing and tending his rose garden in simple circumstances. Even in office Nkrumah, although adopting an extravagant political style, remained modest, almost ascetic, in his private life. His relaxations were not wining and dining but the conversation of intelligent companions. His will left all his possessions to his political party and asked that his wife and children be properly cared for by the party. In contrast to this his military successors in the Ghana presidency sought private fortunes and were subsequently executed for embezzlement.

Perhaps one of the most significant legacies of Nkrumah to all of Africa was his commitment to eroding the ethnic frontiers. "Tribalism" he had seen as a great stumbling block to national achievement. To some, tribalism was an historic phenomenon, rooted in the deep past, while to others, it was a by-product of colonialism, a handy framework for alien administration. Nkrumah's vision of the African past was more grandiose, with an emphasis on trade and empire rather than on community and lineage. But ethnic identities, however deep- or shallow-rooted, however fluctuating in their boundaries and alliances, were nevertheless a reality. Nkrumah transcended them by creating a sense of nation, of pride, of achievement and destiny, which affected all Ghanaians, even those who opposed his own leadership and would have liked to guide Ghana in other directions under other saviors. After Nkrumah had fallen and the cocoa boom had waned, after the exhilaration of success had given way to poverty and disillusion, "tribalism" took on a powerful new political dimension in Ghana. Without a national vision to inspire them, people turned to their local community, their family lineages, their co-religionists, their fellow-speakers of the vernacular, in a new search for security. The Convention People's Party may not have been the ideal vehicle for transcending tribal barriers, but it had managed to do so better than any alternative successor. Even the army, which should have been informed by a professional *esprit de corps* and loyalty to the nation, proved to be a victim of ethnic jealousies which disrupted the path of nationhood and accentuated the fragmentation that accompanied Nkrumah's departure.

The internal reassessment of Nkrumah's contribution to the history of Ghana a quarter of a century after his overthrow must involve an attempt to look at the history of the country after his departure. The achievements and failures of each successor regime are the best yardstick for understanding what Nkrumah tried to do, what he managed to do, and what he failed to do. The first administration to follow Nkrumah was the military regime which overthrew him. Much of its political energy was devoted to trying to legitimize its own position by proclaiming the illegitimacy of Nkrumah. Many sticks were found with which to beat him. He was accused, with some justice, of having abrogated democracy by failing to hold a valid parliamentary election in the ten years which followed the British-run election of 1956. Nevertheless the presidential election of 1960 appeared to demonstrate that Nkrumah could continue to govern with the consent of the people and no military regime tried to demonstrate even that degree of electoral support. Soldiers came to rely on the popular acclaim of sycophants in just the manner they had objected to before.

Military and police accusations of corruption against Nkrumah's associates were partly grounded on firm evidence, but the new rulers showed immediate partiality in the charges they brought. The army was dependent for its ability to govern on the very sectors of society which had been most deeply implicated in private profiteering, namely the civil service and the managerial class in state-controlled industry and commerce. The targets for accusation, therefore, had to be selectively chosen from among members of the establishment who were most expendable, or most visibly owed their prominence to party favors.

Jealousy of preferment rather than morality of purpose was the keynote to the army's purges. The deputy chairman of the new government was the head of the police who had long been familiar with special branch embezzlement files and could use them to enforce cooperation by bureaucratic malefactors rather than to advance the rule of law. Casting stones at Nkrumah's extra-judicial behavior fitted the new rulers ill. Cooperation between army leaders and civilian bureaucrats had an impact on the ideology of the new regime. It was a conservative government, rewarding success rather than ministering to need, with a voice very different from that of Nkrumah. The entrenched realities of Ghana's politics, however, meant that policy, ideology, and personality had only very limited effect and could no longer significantly shift the national course of one small postcolonial republic.

This inability of government to influence national trends was particularly demonstrated by the second civilian government which attempted to determine the fate of the country in the years after Nkrumah. This 1969 government was elected in a ballot which was probably as free and fair as those which Nkrumah had won in the colonial period. The new prime minister was Kofi Busia, the old scholar-politician returned from exile. After twenty-one years of criticizing Nkrumah he had at last discovered just how narrow was the room for maneuver at the top. Busia had two uncomfortable supports to his government. One was the army which "refereed" his politics in much the way that Arden-Clarke had refereed Nkrumah's politics in the 1950s. The second was the regional and ethnic alliance which had supported him in 1956 when he tried to play the devolutionist card against Nkrumah. Busia's old political allies returned to his side in 1969 expecting favors for regional interests. The rise of ethnic consciousness on the Ghana political scene was rapid and divisive. In other African countries ethnic loyalty, security, and benefits had been significant during and after the colonial period. Now they spread to Ghana where Nkrumah had hitherto kept them in abeyance.

The rival ethnic powers in post-Nkrumah Ghana were the Asante who supported Busia and the eastern Ewé who opposed him and counted among their number the police strong-man and Nkrumah's old lieutenant, Gbedemah, who had been in exile since 1961. The Busia civilians had been no more successful than the army or Nkrumah in freeing Ghana from international controls. The decision which spelt their downfall was an externally recommended decision to devalue the currency. Illegitimate notice of the decision was leaked to the government's friends who got their money away and stock-piled goods before the 45 percent devaluation hit prices. Young army officers decided that corruption and the perversion of privilege had gone too far. The second Ghana military coup was led by Colonel Akyeampong who swept Busia away in 1972.

The failure of Busia to right the wrongs of the Nkrumah years caused surprise and a need to reassess the record. The international professor-politician was able to speak to the world in sober terms, but Ghanaians wanted to return to the glorious days when they were led by a statesman of Nkrumah's stature who spoke in ringing tones of authority. At home the Busia coalition spoke with an academic tongue but soon discovered that politics was rough and rapidly began to play accordingly. Busia, like Nkrumah, was too weak in resisting the demands of his associates for rewards and too strong in resisting his opponents. His constitutional purity, which had been so offended by Nkrumah's assault on the independence of the judiciary, rapidly waned when he too found the legal system clipped his political wings. In a trial of strength the prime minister savagely attacked the judges and demonstrated as profound an intolerance of opposition as Nkrumah had done.

The enemies of the Busia era turned out to be the same as the enemies of the Nkrumah regime, both left and right. The greatest protest came from the farmers. It was cocoa farmers who had been the source of most external wealth for the country, but their wealth continued to be drained off to satisfy the wants of urban dwellers, civic employees, politicians, development planners, and merchants who had received benefits from a program of selling off state corporations. Food farmers were also despairing of their future when foreign exchange was used to buy imported food rather than build up the transport system to carry local foods and increase investment in agriculture at large. But if farmers were the old allies of the Busia politicians who were now neglected and alienated, an equally potent source of opposition came from the urban wage-earners. They had been the heroes of Nkrumah's early socialism, but had rapidly found that their wages did not keep pace with living costs in a society where the privileged had power and the state wanted to abrogate all the revenue it could for long-term or prestige investments. The workers, and their merchant wives, demonstrated long and loud at the decline of their fortunes under Nkrumah, celebrated his overthrow by the military, voted for the civilian government that the army commended to them, but rapidly found that they were no better off under Nkrumah's official opposition than they had been under Nkrumah himself. Busia became as unpopular in two years as Nkrumah had become in fifteen. The blame should not have been personalized but in Ghana, as in most of Africa, politics is put in personal rather than ideological terms. Nkrumah had tried to theorize the predicament of a small country with a badly managed economy victim of world pressures, but to most voters the issue was the man not the predicament. Busia was no more able than Nkrumah to alter course on fundamental issues but was similarly blamed. Moreover, the accusations rapidly began to pour in from his heartland constituency, the modern élite. Expectations had been high among the educated and affluent but instead they found jobs being curtailed, imports being restricted, taxes being increased in an austerity program that was reasonable but politically unpopular. There was no lament for Nkrumah's opponents when they lost power in January 1972.

The army regime of Colonel Akyeampong took power, like all armies, to satisfy its own interests. Both Busia and Nkrumah failed to understand the essential rule of civilian politics that armies must be given status and reward if they are to be distanced from political ambition. The new army government aimed to return to the golden days of Nkrumah which, after six years of alternative austerity, re-emerged as an era of greatness. The past was rehabilitated, socialism ceased to be a term of abuse, farming was given a new pre-eminence. The second army regime, like the first, hoped to be able to redirect the ship of state and then hand over to civilians, though this time to ones in the Nkrumah mold rather than the Busia mold. They found, however, that the fruits of office were too sweet. Like all their predecessors, populists, policemen, intellectuals, they succumbed to corrupt favors. In particular the army perverted the trade in cocoa by privately selling part of the crop for hard currency to the neighboring "French" territories rather than using the revenue for national reconstruction. The army itself eventually turned Akyeampong out of office and planned a return to civilian rule. A half-Scottish flight-lieutenant, Gerry Rawlings, undertook a "house-cleansing" operation in which the most obviously corrupt of the soldier-politicians were brutally removed. This paved the way, a mere seven years after Nkrumah's death, for the return to power of Nkrumah associates in a reasonably free election. Rawlings, however, kept a watchful eye on their political activities and when they seemed no more able than others to rescue the country from the competing factions of the urban bourgeoisie, he turned them out to establish a "technocracy" with himself in charge. Corruption may have been reduced, but dependency on the outside world was not. In 1979 the oil crisis hit Ghana harshly. In 1983 the Volta dam ran dry in the great drought and the aluminum smelters had to suspend production. Ghana remained a victim of natural calamity and of world conspiracy. But it was still the pioneer of African freedom, and its founder, Nkrumah, was still remembered as the first black politician to tread the world stage.

5

Nkrumah in Retirement

Kwame Nkrumah arrived in Guinea on 2 March 1966 to begin five years of retirement from the presidency of Ghana. He was welcomed by his host, Sékou Touré, with a twenty-one gun salute and an invitation to become honorary co-president of his chosen country of exile. He had been deposed from office six days earlier by the Ghana police, who had feared an investigation of their corrupt practices, and the Ghana army, who had feared being mobilized for active service in Rhodesia. It had fallen to his hapless Chinese host, Zhou en Lai, to inform Nkrumah of the Ghana *coup d'état* and arrange his rapid departure for Conakry, where he was installed in a modest villa on the seashore and given round-the-clock protection by a few dozen gendarmes.

The most striking feature of Nkrumah's early years of retirement was his good humor. The boyish sense of fun, the exuberant enthusiasms, the naïve enjoyment of new ideas and sensations, all returned to him once the burdens of office had been lifted. He missed the small zoo at Flagstaff House, but enjoyed the pussycat who nestled under his desk. He laughed at his own clumsy attempts to learn to drive a car. He reassured his friends that he would be able to find means of providing adequate nutrition amidst alien austerity and claimed that his health had never been better. He sharpened his mind by regular games of chess at lunch-time. He kept fit by continuing to play tennis. He skipped about his compound, shadow-boxing and laughing. He indulged in endless daydreams about his return to politics and maintained a huge correspondence with friends and admirers of a lifetime, though he received comparatively few visitors and was extremely reluctant to be interviewed. He continued to long for the companionship of intelligent women, as he had done throughout his life. He made efforts to learn French and regularly entertained Madame Sékou Touré, even agreeing to dance the highlife with her at a ball although such gregarious celebration was not his custom. He took a great interest in his garden and carefully planted his roses in white pots with named labels. He longed for orange marmalade and arranged for his cook to learn how to make it and thereby supplement his supply from England. And he wrote frequently and with tender fondness to his maternal confidante and intellectual amanuensis, June Milne, who edited and published his correspondence in a Panaf edition entitled *Kwame Nkrumah: The Conakry Years—His Life and Letters*.

Nkrumah's reading during his exile was far-ranging in its diversity. He showed an interesting reluctance to give opinions of his own on many subjects and sometimes asked his correspondents what they thought of the books he was reading before passing judgment himself. In January 1969 he was reading a book on rocketry, the autobiographies of Oswald Mosley the British fascist, Kim Philby the spy-master, and Senator Fulbright, Cleage's *The Black Messiah*, Simone de Beauvoir's *The Second Sex*, Pomeroy's *Guerrilla Warfare and Marxism*, and he was seeking a copy of Wilfred Burchett's *Pourquoi le Vietnam Gagne*, which he was willing to tackle in French. He had happily received a gift copy of the Oxford dictionary of quotations. He refused on the other hand to review Thomas Hodgkin's *festschrift* for the Balliol College magazine, claiming that he had not got the literary resources at his disposal to write a searching and scholarly review. What Nkrumah did read with some degree of systematic persistence was material on military history, beginning with Mao Tse-tung's work on guerrilla warfare. His overthrow by the military, whose psychology he had so conspicuously failed to understand while in office, gave him one clear incentive. He was also concerned, however, to think about how the military could be used in future to free Africa of foreign influence.

Shortly before he was overthrown, Nkrumah had apparently prepared at least an outline draft of a manual on guerrilla warfare. Copies of such a manual were seemingly distributed by his enemies as proof of his subversive attitude to his fellow presidents in Africa. The original had purportedly been given to General Barwah, Nkrumah's then newly appointed chief of staff who was murdered in the coup that overthrew Nkrumah and brought General Ankrah back to command of the Ghana army. The draft handbook on warfare may even have been one of the items of evidence that caused the Ghana army to fear that Nkrumah might put them on active duty again, as he had painfully done in the Congo crisis of 1960. Be that as it may, Nkrumah arrived in Conakry and set himself the task of re-inventing and revising his ideas for a draft manual on warfare. Although he had at least one secretary who could take dictation and type letters and drafts for him, he apparently did most of his writing by hand, complaining piteously when an infected finger made writing painful. His letter to June Milne on the subject of his military handbook is revealing of his literary method. It indicates that he outlined the ideas he wanted fleshed out, and then got an associate to do a full draft, which he could edit to his own predilections. His instructions for turning the outline of the manual into a text, personally typed by his literary executrix with two fingers, were as follows:

> Now shall I say a little bit about the *Manual*? Study it
> carefully. You can see that it is highly compressed. And it
> shouldn't be so. I was trying to put many things into a nut-
> shell, but you can expand them. Divide and group them
> into chapters. I could have done more on the role of
> women in the African people's revolutionary struggle with
> particular reference to the All-African People's Revolutionary
> Army. Many points and sections could be expanded and
> elaborated. The part dealing with party organization could
> be expanded. What we need to complement the AAPRA is
> an all Pan African unifying party. This could be called the
> All-African People's Socialist Party and must be planned on
> a Pan African basis with the AAPRA as its military arm, one
> supplementing the other. The AAPRA and the AAPSP
> should supersede the OAU and make it redundant.
>
> I have not dealt much with the settler regimes in Africa,
> e.g. Rhodesia and South Africa. These are as much aspects
> of racialism, or racism, as its economic or political motives.
> Settler regimes must be exposed and fought against. I have
> casually dealt with this is *Africa Must Unite*. Look it up. In
> *Consciencism* I never developed the Islamic philosophy for
> emancipation. This can be developed in the *Manual*. We
> must break through religious superstitions. Religion can be
> given a scientific basis, and it can be made scientific if de-
> void of its mumbo-jumbo devices. See if you can find
> books on Islamic philosophy and/or history. If you find

any let me have copies. There are one or two but I have
forgotten their titles and authors. Any book on them will
do. On the whole we can make great improvement on the
Manual.[10]

Rarely can a ghost-writer have been given such a free hand, such
peremptory instructions, and such a cavalier approach to the choice of
source materials. To add to her difficulties the project was veiled in the
utmost secrecy, and even when completed, publication was delayed lest
accusations of subversion hinder rather than enhance Nkrumah's chance
of regaining power. The letter of instructions is informative, however,
since it tends to confirm the generally held view that Nkrumah himself
was never a great writer. His slim volume on *Colonial Freedom,* although
written before 1945, was not widely published until 1962, and his 1957
Autobiography, although sternly controlled by him in telephone calls to
his publisher in Edinburgh, was actually written by Erica Powell.
Nkrumah's philosophical work was the product of a study group in
which he participated, rather than the fruits of solitary thought. His
earlier concern with philosophy was maintained during his retirement
years. On the day Bertrand Russell died he dropped a rose petal into the
sea in his memory and resolved to read again the autobiography he had
recently received to rediscover Russell's "search for knowledge and his
pity for suffering mankind." Nkrumah was apparently aware that his
own ghosted efforts to present a coherent philosophy in *Consciencism*
had not been very successful. He encouraged June Milne to write, under
her own name, a book on *Nkrumaism:*

You will have to do a bit of reading in philosophy. You
see my whole thinking and action is derived from a synthe-
sis of the materialism of Feuerbach, the dialectical idealism

of Hegel, Darwin's theory of evolution, and the dialectical materialism of Marx. Out of these I have tried to evolve a philosophy of my own. I tried to do this in *Consciencism*. How much I succeeded I don't know. Active political life has not given me the time to think more about this.

You see, the materialism of Feuerbach recognizes no truths except those of power and matter; the idealistic philosophy of Hegel, or rather the Hegelian dialectics which presupposes nothing constant but change and movement. . . . Then the evolution theory of Darwin which reduced man from the image of God to that of the biologically developed animal. Man with his unlimited capacity for good and evil. Then the dialectical formulation of Marx and Engels which repudiates any divine influence in the affairs of men and in which truth is measured by the pressure of conditions and circumstances of a special situation. It is these which have been shaping my thinking and thoughts. But I also believe that there is a source of all power in the universe. I liken that power to, say, electricity or atomic energy, millions of times more powerful. This is the sustenance of all that there is. When you come we shall talk more about this. My time is running out and I must leave you now.[11]

Drafting book outlines on neocolonialism was not the only aspect of Nkrumah's publishing interest. He had been instrumental in setting up a news magazine called *Africa and the World* which had been established in London in 1964 by the Bureau of African Affairs, a semi-covert branch of the Accra government. The magazine was edited by Douglas Rogers and published by John Marshment who had been

British employees of the government press in Ghana and who continued work for Nkrumah after the coup cut off state funding. Nkrumah provided a subsidy from his book royalty account in London and received both editor and publisher at his villa soon after his arrival in Guinea. Of even greater importance to his cause, however, was the establishment of Panaf Books, a company owned by himself and managed by June Milne, which reprinted Nkrumah books that commercial publishers did not keep in print and published first editions of the works that were launched in his name while he was in Guinea.

In Guinea a sense of direction, purpose, and urgency was maintained in Nkrumah's office by constant contact with the post office and the airport. International flights were of the utmost interest to the exile. When politics stopped Pan American Airways from calling at Conakry this was a source of concern regardless of Nkrumah's ambivalent attitude toward the United States and all its works in Africa. When economic realities led to the suspension of the direct KLM flights to Amsterdam and Europe, the office routine was disrupted and the sense of isolation increased. When days of heavy rain stopped the flight from France, Nkrumah rejoiced in the drama of Africa's weather but worried about his lifeline to the world outside. When diplomats were seized from a Nigerian Airways flight on the coastal run there was righteous anger in the office. Because mail was unreliable, and because urgency had to be felt, some communication took place by telegraph. The account book, if any were kept, of the running costs of Nkrumah's office and household would make fascinating reading not only for the sources of income it might reveal, but also for the outgoings that it might record. When the mails did arrive there was rejoicing among all the entourage of the exiled "court." Nkrumah opened his parcels with the glee of a child—books, sweets, foods, medicines, and best of all new editions of his own works from his own press installed in half an office in London's Regent Street.

Celebrations were important to the exiles. Although Nkrumah had largely put his Catholic childhood, and his student days as a Protestant preacher, behind him he nevertheless celebrated Christmas. His household rehearsed hymns and carols to sing to him. His view of God emerged, curiously, from the rare reading of a novel, Cronin's *The Keys of the Kingdom,* where the phrase "O God, dear God, give me humility, and give me faith" caused him to reflect that humility elevates and faith conquers. His spiritual discipline involved fasting on Fridays, and when his Muslim colleagues adopted the ascetic lenten practices of Ramadan he joined them. He was curiously pleased and flattered to receive a handwritten Christmas card from Edgar Kaiser, the American tycoon who had built Nkrumah's great hydroelectric dam on the Volta River, though he hastily added that "I never wish to be a millionaire! Millionaires live on the backs of poor people and call it business." In addition to Christmas, birthdays were an important part of the morale-raising routine of retirement and although the date of Nkrumah's birthday is not known his official birthday was celebrated and cards were received from the now widely scattered personnel that had staffed his most cherished projects concerning African unity and African socialism. His wife and children never visited him in exile but remained distant figures in Cairo who only occasionally impinge on his apologetically neglectful correspondence, as when he wrote to Madame Fathia to make sure the children were eating plenty of honey.

Nkrumah's close association with many British friends, colleagues, admirers, and critics was reflected in the extensive correspondence that he carried on in retirement. One of his early and rare visitors in Conakry was Geoffrey Bing, the British lawyer and politician who had been his attorney general. Bing reported his suspicion that one of the police plotters who had overthrown Nkrumah, and locked Bing up, had been involved in diamond racketeering. Bing also reported on the attempts in Britain to put the record of Nkrumah's presidency in a more favorable light than that which pervaded the media. Bing even offered to help Nkrumah draft replies to written interview questions to be published in the conservative *Daily Telegraph,* but Nkrumah refused. He also refused to be interviewed by the BBC and was critical of Bing for having reported so fully on his own visit to him in Guinea. Nkrumah read British press cuttings avidly, grumbled about Bridget Bloom in the *Financial Times,* made disparaging remarks about David Williams of *West Africa* magazine, gave thanks for the writings of Thomas Hodgkin, and expressed his ambivalence about Fenner Brockway who "always speaks as if he is my mentor" and who "makes me sick: the same old paternalism." His isolation was enhanced when he rather petulantly and somewhat guiltily refused to see either Basil Davidson, the historian of African liberation, or U Thant, the secretary-general of the United Nations, on their visits to Guinea.

Although Nkrumah's relations with his Guinea hosts are portrayed in his selected correspondence as cordial, his belief that French-speaking African leaders were less pure in their nationalism than his own British-oriented followers continued to be striking. On 29 October 1969 he wrote to June Milne: "Have just finished reading Mortimer's *France and the Africans.* Not deep stuff, just the story of black Africans and their excolonial masters. One thing it does show up is the mentality of these French Africans nationalists—all bourgeois-oriented to France. . . . Did I tell you that I am short of raisins? I would like four packets." Nkrumah would apparently not have described as "bourgeois orientation towards London" his close cultural attachment to Britain, and his excellent colloquial command of English, but the distinction between French assimilation and British assimilation in Africa can be hard for the neutral observer to discern. Although he frequently ranted against British policies and politicians, his love affair with Britain continued throughout his retirement and his references to Queen Elizabeth II continued to portray her as his fairy godmother. The respect was apparently mutual. British friends were not the only ones to keep Nkrumah supplied with Red Cross-type parcels and bring comfort to the austerity of his retirement. He offered his guests brown sugar sent by Fidel Castro and fresh mangoes flown from Cairo by Gamal Nasser. In a rather more bizarre fashion he received messages of support from former heads of government in the Commonwealth, including the autocratic right-wing prime minister of Singapore, Lee Kuan Yew. Some of his closest correspondents were black Americans. It was generally supposed that Nkrumah had lived a lonely life during the Great Depression in Pennsylvania, but in fact he maintained or restored contact with some of his friends of that era. He also spent much time dwelling on his close friendship with W. E. B. Du Bois, who had left America to settle in Ghana and had been buried in the grounds of Nkrumah's castle-home at Christiansborg. Du Bois's last project, sponsored by Nkrumah, was the *Encyclopaedia Africana*, of which two volumes were eventually published by Keith Irvine, a British editor whose parents had worked at Achimota School in the 1920s and who had served on Nkrumah's staff at the United Nations after independence. Du Bois's widow, Shirley, was one of Nkrumah's most regular correspondents when she was stranded in Cairo, deprived of her Ghanaian citizenship by the military junta. She supplied him with food parcels through the diplomatic bag and caused him to complain ungenerously about the red tape and bureaucracy France had bequeathed to Guinea. She eventually moved to Beijing and outlived Nkrumah by several years, but long before that he had become impatient with her stream of advice and independence of spirit. On 14 February 1969 he wrote to her somewhat sharply:

> I am a little surprised at you for suggesting that I should accept an offer to teach. You do not seem to know me yet. You forget that I am a professional revolutionary: the gun without the pen is useless and the pen without the gun is even more useless. My way lies in Action and Struggle. And in struggling and performing these actions, I can teach others in that way. Unlike W. E. B. I believe not in life but in action, not in people as people but in revolutionary action to save people from man's inhumanity to man.[12]

Health was always one of Nkrumah's concerns. At the height of his career as prime minister he used to worry that he might catch a cold in the head, a fear he once expressed during his weekly interview with the Earl of Listowel, the Queen's representative in Ghana and Nkrumah's head of state in the early years of independence. In exile his health caused him much anxiety. He ordered jars of wheat germ and tins of black treacle by post, once with very sticky consequences. He also tried to ship out from London an orthopedic bed for his back. He was concerned to get up-to-date malaria tablets for his household and ephedrine tablets for an asthmatic member of staff. One of his biggest crises occurred when his long-standing cook, who had always accompanied him on his travels round the world, developed liver failure and died. He feared not only that he would not get an adequately balanced diet, a subject on which he had been coached by Erica Powell during her long years as his friend and secretary, but worse still that the chaotic staffing arrangements in his kitchen might allow malefactors to poison him. He took to hoarding food in a tuck cupboard in his spartan room.

Nkrumah frequently asserted that he was fully informed about events in Ghana during his exile. His expectation of economic and political collapse and his recall as the "savior," Osagyefo, had a strong element of wishful thinking. One of his British correspondents, Pat Sloane of the staff of the Winneba Ideological Institute, wrote him an honest letter describing the lack of support that could be detected for him after his overthrow, but still Nkrumah strained to catch every straw in the wind that might indicate that he could soon be on his way back to Accra. Although the first military regime and the succeeding Busia civilian government were neither efficient nor untainted by malpractice, it was only in the 1970s, after Nkrumah's death, that drought and food shortages, rising oil prices and the collapse of transport, the flight of the professional class to better paid positions in Nigeria and Britain, the large-scale smuggling of cocoa to the "French" neighbors, and the venal growth of embezzlement in the army, led Ghanaians to recall the "golden" days of Nkrumah and restore some of his domestic ideas to their political agenda.

The end of Nkrumah's retirement came in a series of catastrophes. In his villa he felt increasingly beleaguered and suspected foreign agents of tampering with his mails. He became ever more security conscious and feared that he might be abducted or assassinated. His health was no longer a subject to spasmodic fever and hypochondria but became seriously impaired by lumbago or other genuine complaints. He tried to obtain a layman's medical dictionary and ordered drugs and painkillers from England. He considered arranging a trip to the Soviet Union for a health check, noting nevertheless that the plan would of course be aborted if "the balloon went up" and he were recalled to Ghana to resume his presidential career. But the great blow came in November 1970 when Portuguese commandos invaded Guinea aiming to abduct Amilcar Cabral — the leading philosophical and military opponent of

Portuguese rule in Africa—and to destroy the Conakry haven that protected Portugal's colonial opponents who had come from neighboring Bissau. Nkrumah took refuge in the North Korean embassy lest the invasion be designed not only to destroy anti-Portuguese bases but also to obliterate Nkrumah, that other prominent anti-colonial exile in Conakry. The invasion may have had the even more ambitious object of overthrowing the presidency of Sékou Touré. Touré himself believed that the abortive attack had been an orchestrated attempt on his own life and, moreover, that it had been condoned by fifth-columnists among his own party faithful and his own state employees. Nkrumah, who had ruled Ghana for fifteen years without a single political execution, was forced to witness a treason trial of over a hundred people and to attend an hysterical political rally where the purge was acclaimed. Thereafter Nkrumah's health declined ever more rapidly and in August 1971 he was secretly flown on a stretcher to a clinic in Bucharest. He died of cancer eight months later.

NOTES

1. Dennis Austin, *Ghana Observed* (Manchester, 1976), pp. 12–13.

2. Sir Charles Arden-Clarke to his family, 27 March 1955, cited in Richard Rathbone, "The Transfer of Power in Ghana, 1945–57" (Ph.D. thesis, University of London, 1968), p. 241.

3. James Moxon, *Volta: Man's Greatest Lake,* 2d ed. (London: André Deutsch, 1984), p. 271.

4. Kwame Nkrumah, *Ghana: The Autobiography of Kwame Nkrumah* (New York: Thomas Nelson and Sons, 1957), pp. xv–xvi.

5. Jeff Crisp, *The Story of an African Working Class* (London: Zed, 1984), p. 96.

6. Ibid., p. 134.

7. Ruth First, *The Barrel of a Gun: Political Power in Africa and the Coup d'État* (London: Allen Lane, 1970), pp. 363–407.

8. David Rooney, *Kwame Nkrumah* (London: I. B. Tauris, 1988), pp. 258–59.

9. H. T. Alexander, *African Tightrope* (London: Pall Mall, 1965), pp. 33–49.

10. June Milne, *Kwame Nkrumah: The Conraky Years—His Life and Letters* (London: Zed, 1990), pp. 72–73.

11. Ibid., p. 169.

12. Ibid., p. 294.

SELECTED BIBLIOGRAPHY

Marika Sherwood, *Kwame Nkrumah: The Years Abroad, 1935-1947* (Accra-Legon: Freedom Publications, 1996), the most recent biographical work on Nkrumah, provides a corrective to Nkrumah's own "autobiographical" memory of his motives and activities.

June Milne, *Kwame Nkrumah: The Conakry Years—His Life and Letters* (London: Zed, 1990), by the manager of Panaf Books, provides insight into the years of Nkrumah's retirement.

David Rooney, *Kwame Nkrumah: The Political Kingdom in the Third World* (London: I. B. Tauris, 1988) is a thorough political biography. Rooney has also written a biography of *Sir Charles Arden-Clarke* (London: Rex Collings, 1982).

Erica Powell, *Private Secretary (Female) Gold Coast* (London: Hurst, 1984) is a non-political personal portrait of Nkrumah by his secretary who also largely wrote his autobiography, *Ghana* (Edinburgh, New York, London: Thomas Nelson and Sons, 1957).

Kwame Nkrumah, *Revolutionary Path* (London: Panaf, 1973) is a collection of Nkrumah's speeches and essays, including his first essay "Towards Colonial Freedom." Fifteen books published in Nkrumah's name are in print.

Dennis Austin, *Politics in Ghana, 1945-60* (London: Oxford, 1964) is the classic study of the period by a scholar-witness who published two other outstanding works on Ghana.

Richard Rathbone, "The Transfer of Power in Ghana, 1945-1957" (London, 1968) is an unpublished doctoral thesis with a rich documentation and an even-handed academic assessment.

Tony Killick, *Development Economics in Action: A Study of Economic Policies in*

Ghana (London: Heinemann, 1978) provides a succinctly convincing interpretation of Nkrumah's economic strategies by a British scholar.

R. Hyam, "Africa and the Labour Government" in Andrew Porter and Robert Holland (eds.), *Theory and Practice in the History of European Expansion Overseas* (London: Cass, 1988) provides a recent assessment of the British connection.

George Padmore, *The Gold Coast Revolution* (London: Dobson, 1953) is an early account by a Caribbean journalist-participant.

Richard Wright, *Black Power* (London: Dobson, 1954) is a perceptive insight by a surprised black American visitor.

Geoffrey Bing, *Reap the Whirlwind* (London: MacGibbon & Kee, 1968) is a positive retrospective by Nkrumah's British attorney-general.

A. A. Afrifa, *The Ghana Coup* (London: Cass, 1966) contains the self-justification of one of the military plotters.

Henry L. Bretton, *The Rise and Fall of Kwame Nkrumah* (London: Pall Mall, 1967) is a negative interpretation by an American academic in the immediate aftermath of Nkrumah's fall.

Yuri Smertin, *Kwame Nkrumah* (Moscow: Progress Publishers, 1987) is a Soviet re-evaluation twenty years on.

John Dunn (ed.), *West African States* (Cambridge, 1978) contains a comparison of Nkrumah and his successors by Richard Rathbone.

Jeff Crisp, *The Story of an African Working Class* (London: Zed, 1984) analyzes Nkrumah's relations with the miners.

Richard Jeffries, *Class, Power and Ideology in Ghana* (Cambridge, 1978) is a serious scholarly analysis based on the study of the railwaymen.

Colin Legum, *Pan-Africanism* (London: Pall Mall, 1962) contains a rich harvest of contemporary documentation.

Willis Bell, *Ghana on the Move* contains some fine photographs.

James Moxon, *Volta: Man's Greatest Lake,* 2d ed. (London: André Deutsch, 1984) is a thorough P.R. job on Nkrumah's biggest economic venture.

INDEX

ABOUT THE AUTHOR

DAVID BIRMINGHAM is Professor of Modern History at the University of Kent at Canterbury. He is a British graduate of the University of Ghana who lived intermittently in that country for much of the Nkrumah era. His book *The Decolonization of Africa* was published by Ohio University Press in 1995. The third volume of *A History of Central Africa* (edited jointly with Phyllis Martin) was published by Longman in 1998.

Printed in the USA
CPSIA information can be obtained
at www.ICGtesting.com
LVHW091355161023
760974LV00001B/3